Angels Do Come -
JUST CALL!

KATE O'KANE

authorHOUSE®

AuthorHouse™
1663 Liberty Drive
Bloomington, IN 47403
www.authorhouse.com
Phone: 1-800-839-8640

First published by AuthorHouse   02/13/2012

ISBN: 978-1-4678-8387-0 (sc)
ISBN: 978-1-4678-8388-7 (ebk)

Contents

Everyone has a story— Everyone has at least one Angel!

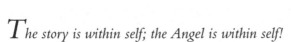

The story is within self; the Angel is within self!

Yes, everyone has a story; no life can be complete without a series of events which create the chapters of one's story. Some chapters are easy; some chapters are full and challenging and others grafted together with various events which colour one's life in various textures; tough, rough, smooth, and soft, painted in colours dark and dim, light and bright. Scenes framed exhibiting the mix of events, encounters and experiences which reflect the inner self.

Within the realm of Christianity we are all bequeathed the gift of at least one Spiritual being to guard and protect us on our journey. Therefore, it is true that everyone has an Angel, a spiritual aide sent by God to support us through the earthly journey we encounter, as we take on the human experience. Angels will only assist or intervene when called upon. In doing so, they will enable the links of the ongoing story to be secured.

Within, the spiritual dimension of life and living, Reality is life. Life is reality, irrespective of the story of life and the cover it wears. Truth and untruth coincide as behind the smiling greeting of those we meet there may be a broken heart. How many of us wear the face of a clown and hide the pain within? Even within the finest garments and the upright assertive form there may lie a heart of stone; or within the image strong and tough there may lie a mind tormented, weak or strong fighting for survival . . . can you identify with this?

Therefore, it is fair to suggest amid all the covers we all share a common thread, that of the story we strive to live accompanied by the Angels who endeavour to bring forth the truth. God's messengers desire to enhance and improve one's wellbeing.

Consequently, it is an invitation to accept with honour the assistance of God's messengers. We are invited to realise the good within, to acknowledge one's talents and skills and where possible and appropriate, to use such to help to make the world in which we live an even greater place, created and designed by God as a place where one's unique contribution and responsibility of self give way to serenity.

Angels have a valuable role to play in this evolution and we have a wealth of diversities to encourage us to participate in this universal spiritual challenge. Therefore, the basic invitation is open to all:

'Angels do come—just call!'

Introduction

Within contemporary society there is a careful and somewhat tentative acceptance towards the perception that within our more progressive culture there is a general belief that what we want, we will acquire; it is a case that we not only must have but we must get what we want right away!

There is a growing sense and subsequent need for instant satisfaction, gratification and indulgence, but this belief and practice does not necessarily bring about the common goal of achieving personal inner peace and ultimate wholeness of self and well-being. Therefore, we are challenged to ask are we living in a world of idealism or realism; is this notion of achieving wholeness of self an accessible goal or is such perceived as a futile phenomenon?

For those who embrace the concept of 'healing' it is fair to suggest that people are open to learning and are therefore beginning to utilise the self-help mechanisms on offer. With the advent and the awareness of alternative approaches to life and living, a greater openness and acceptance to self help tools and therapies are more readily recognised and worthy of consideration. When such tools and instruments yield to make life better when appropriated in a base of Christianity and Faith, all paths to wholeness are embraced.

Angel therapy, reflexology, acupuncture, are examples of some of the valuable alternative and complementary tools available to achieving a more balanced life. In relation to religious traditions including Christianity, Buddhism and Judaism prayer is a powerful source of support; prayer in various forms such as meditation, contemplation, Lectio Divina and devotional prayer are tools which help to nourish the soul. The Scared Scriptures, the Psalms offer guidance and spiritual direction.

Such approaches are becoming more apparent contributors in relation to ultimate well-being. Therefore, various therapies, instruments and procedures alongside traditional methods or alone, complement and provide alternative healing of body, mind and soul.

Physical healing contributes to the healing of the soul and mind and vice versa. Healing cannot occur without a transformation; healing occurs when one is prepared to receive. The process requires patience and openness to acceptance of what is for one's highest good. Any form of healing, miracle or cure takes time, patience and the belief that what is for one's highest good is paramount to a successful and appropriate effect. There is no doubt that for some people healing does occur, miracles do happen.

In such cases, so much depends on the nature of the condition, the illness or issue in question. In the final analysis that which is for the highest good of the individual may not necessarily reflect what is perceived as an appropriate answer to the want or desire of the one in need. There is no prayer unanswered; granted the answer may not reflect the profound request but there is always something good to be found. What we do experience is so valuable, much more valuable than one can ever imagine.

We may think we haven't gotten that which we asked for; but in essence it will be clear that the answer came in a form that is for one's highest good.

Trust!

In time we receive the faith and acceptance which helps to cushion any pain to be endured. Blessed with a quiet calmness which helps in the preparation to being open to accept even that which we may never have envisaged, or indeed may ever have thought of!

Grace comes to those who wait, trust and believe!

Therefore, while we cannot deny that instant healing is possible, we need to accept that healing of body, mind and soul is more likely to occur as a result of an ongoing process that involves a number of factors: including prayer, traditional and conventional medicine, alternative and complementary approaches to well-being, to clarity and empowerment of thought, inner peace and an openness towards the acceptance and awareness of the utility of prayer and spiritual help. Frequently, we hear that *'near death or out of body experiences occur'*, experiences which were grounded in inexplicable beautiful ways.

Such can enhance the wholeness of self, highlight that which helps to motivate and maintain a balanced way of life and living. While medicines may have a positive effect towards easing the strain and pain of physical and mental illness, complimentary approaches used with and/ or in a spiritual way can offer much to greater flexibility and stability of self. A desired balanced wholeness of body, mind and soul are essentially a reflection of eventual transformation and fulfilment brought forth as a result of ongoing recognition and acceptance of the need to rebuild, restore and revitalise all parts of self.

Recognising the need for complete healing is a first step, but it is important that the healing of the soul is attended to also. When we seek the stability of spirituality, many aspects of Faith offer support, including that of the Angelic realm, a source of spirituality founded in God. So have we begun to realise and accept the importance and need for a well balanced self?

If one part of one's being is not working, inevitably this will have a negative impact on the whole self akin to the domino effect, i.e. when one block falls, the effect is ongoing. With the emergence of a modern secular and somewhat indifferent cultural world, there is a growing personal approach to obtaining and sustaining wholeness of self.

There is a greater awareness, acceptance and appreciation of the power of Angels and the gift of guidance given by God to each one of us. God in His loving kindness has given each of us His gift of an Angel to lovingly assist, to help and to respond to our personal needs, when called upon. As God is immortal, His Angels were created to act on our behalf; Angels do not have the shortcomings of humans; they aim to bring God's peace and calmness into our lives.

Therefore, they, the Angels are akin to a bridge spanning the path between Heaven and Earth. They lovingly listen and communicate to God on our behalf. Ultimately, God wants us to be happy and peaceful.

As the approach to wholeness of well-being has become a challenging and cynical phenomenon for many; a palpable concept for others and an exciting and somewhat romantic theory for some to comprehend, there is the emergence of confusion and desire where realism and idealism of life coincide. Until quite recently emphasis has been assigned more so to the wellbeing of the physical and psychological needs or in essence the body and mind aspects of being.

As a result, the nourishment of the soul, the spirit or the inner self whichever term one assigns to this important part of self, has up until quite recently been somewhat neglected.

Consequently, the apparent lack of support/neglect for spiritual nourishment has begun to be recognised as worthy of being an important element to be included and integrated into the plan towards achieving wholeness of self, and is being accepted and appreciated as an important component towards achieving ultimate well-being.

Angels come!

Angels come; yes, they do: I believe and am aware that Angels exist. This awareness has not just emerged out of nowhere. This awareness has emerged through an opening of self to a new way of thinking and bringing old and new ideas together. Frequently, we hear people say, *'I just go direct, I don't pray to Holy Angels or the Saints. I go straight to the top: I take the direct route to God'*. This seems a little sad. For instance, if we wanted to reach someone, in most cases, it's seems fair to say that we would make contact through a friend, a family member or an acquaintance. The Angels in a way are similar to secretaries or private assistances, PA's. If we want to contact a doctor, a bishop, a consultant, a solicitor, it is through such channels contacts are made. It is the role of such personnel to pass our messages to the top and in turn to reply to our request. So too, the Holy Angels and the Saints intercede on our behalf to the Lord our God—we pray, we trust, we wait.

My awareness of the Angels is as a consequence of my desire to understand the concept of Angelology not just in relation to the New Age school of thought but based in the acceptance and belief of God's gift to me, to you, to all. I didn't want to be taken along a path where God was pushed aside. I wanted to embrace the consciousness of Angels, accepting the good, the bad and the ugly. I was searching for the authentic description of Angels and their functions in relation God's creation of humanity. It was apparent that to acknowledge the Angels, it is important that we realise the three groups: (i) the good Holy Angels who in sheer humility desire to bring us to God and delivering from God that which is for our highest good; (ii) the bad destructive elements who seek to bring destruction and upheaval when we endeavour to do God's will, those who come a disguise of love and gentleness and (iii) the fallen Angels, led by Satan who were banished by God to eternal damnation; they continuously seek to attack those who desire to love and to obey God. Satan hates those who seek God.

Sometimes, it is difficult to distinguish between the good, the bad and the ugly elements which encompass the term Angels. The good Angels do not need to explain themselves; their spiritual ambience is so powerfully serene. However, occasionally, we may encounter people who seem so sweet, so good and so caring and give way to such attributes to find in time the opposite to be revealed. The evil spirits fight for human attention. Yet, in all we find that we have the gift of *'free will'*. We make judgements whether they are right or wrong. We frequently are blinded to the truth; we cannot see the wood for the trees! We cannot understand why God cannot just heal what we know, He knows, to be dis-eased. Yet, we are invited to call upon the Angels who take our concerns directly to God and nudge Him while we wait on His response.

Within Sacred Scripture, so often while recognising the needs of those he met, Jesus asked *"what is it that I can do for you, and/or what is it that you want of me'*. Some may say *'what a question to ask someone he knew was blind or crippled'*. This is a reminder that while God knows our needs, God will not intervene without an invitation. After all, how can God and the Angels intervene when we have received the great gift of *'free will, free choice'?* If we are close to someone and we are in need, we can't expect them to read our minds, can we? We have to speak up and ask for what we need.

Jesus has said: *'Ask and you shall receive; seek and you will find; knock and the door shall be opened unto you!'*

Do not be afraid; ask God for the help, support and protection. Even though God is aware of our every need, He and his messengers respect our use of *'free will'*. Yet, help is always at hand. Be comforted in the knowledge that God knows our needs and desires and wants to help.

Yes!

God knows our needs and desires, so call upon the Angels without delay. Angels are with us, and wait for us to call upon them for support and help. Angels come to us in various ways. Angels of God respond to our call. Angels desire to serve.

I was fascinated when people shared their stories, their amazing experiences and indeed some recollections of very simple happenings which gave such a depth of affirmation to their belief that there has to be some kind of spiritual beings ministering to our needs. With such in mind, I wish to share some simple examples, personal and shared testimonies, antidotes and scriptural references in relation to *'Angels'* and the *'Healing power of the Angels'*.

Angels Come,
Yes they do—do they?

Initially, I personally craved to learn about the Angels, but was weary of what might be revealed to me. Yet, within contemporary society there is an awareness that such a phenomenon is possible and I secretly searched to unravel the myths of the past. The concept surrounding the world of the Angelic Realm has earned a huge amount of interest over recent times.

For many years the whole notion of Angels and the power of the Angels has become a very vibrant and yet somewhat cynical topic of conversation. Among many of the sceptics, I really, really wanted to know about the power of the Angels but like many people lacked the initial courage to publicly declare such an interest.

Why did I have reservations regards the ever emerging public belief in relation to 'Angels'? Basically, I was a little weary because such a phenomenon had been frowned upon and didn't warrant to be considered as a topic of depth, sustenance and/or achievable. I realised that to understand, really understand, I had to become open and ready to adapt. To nourish the soul requires a 'letting-in' of the Holy Spirit and recognising the gift of the messenger of God who waits to serve. In order for the soul to really live it is a case of being adaptable and flexible, ready to embrace change.

The challenge, therefore, is to change and develop, which requires us to dispose of the old and take hold of the new, revealed in Mark 2:18-22

". . . nobody puts new wine into old wineskins; if he does, the wine will burst the skins, and the wine will be lost and the skins too!"

So, what did I do?

I read and read all the material I could get my hands on in relation to the *'Angels'*. With a childish curiosity and excitement mixed with a quiet sense of trepidation I used my limited knowledge to access what I could, by using my computer to source information. I scoured the Internet, the World Wide Web (www) visiting at random, Angel web sites; I searched through Church and various religious web sites for relevant information and reviewed the Scriptures, the sacred *'Word'*. I was overwhelmed by the vast amount of material available. The Angel search was volatile and explosive.

Within my eager quest, first of all there was the need to access the validity and support in relation to the topic of *'Angels'*; secondly, realising that I needed to understand why contemporary society have become so open and appreciative of the active response of the *'Angels'* and thirdly,

I just wanted to be aware and to experience the presence of an Angel or Angels. The amount of visual and textual material prompted me to open myself more and more fully and trustingly to believing in Angels.

I believed that so much written word and personal testimonies had to add up to something good. This was an affirmation that my search was worthwhile. I asked God to direct me.

As God features frequently in the midst of what I had read and frequently featured in the testimonies of hope, of healing and of gratitude which I was told, I knew in my heart and soul that the study of the Angels was an appropriate undertaking. I thought to myself, *'surely this vast amount of information about Angels couldn't all be bad; surely this information which appears to be and frequently makes reference to God must have some legitimacy.'* With God at the basis of my search, I continued to allow the Angels into my life. I really believed that the focus on the heavenly body of Angels, their role as guides and protectors must surely have some relevance to the positive and encouraging accounts of healing and support given by so many people.

Reading and seeking information about the concept of Angels sparked off an awareness highlighting that of a healthy interest in the spiritual ambience of Angels, their function and their assignments to help, which was not just for me but an awakening for many.

Subconsciously, I assumed most people possibly embraced the notion that the Angels are always with us, not in an intrusive way, but in a quiet gentle way. It is in our growing older that we realise that our Angels never left us. We are fortunate to reconnect with them. They hadn't gone away but they were somehow displaced within the realm of life and living. Similar to making friends; often the direction and demands of life and living take us away from friends, we just drift. It is not intentional. There is no plan, such just happens. So too, it may be the case that for many people, the blue print of life is blurred and may cause the relationship between Angels and self, to be disengaged.

How wonderful to renew this relationship with the Angels. *'I was awakened to receive and utilise the gift God had given to me, and I was eager to call upon the Angels, I was anxious to understand the profound messages and images I encountered as I searched for answers and spiritual development. I excitedly thought, Imagine, I have, you have an Angel, and everyone has at least one Angel'.* Continuing on my personal search for information and apt affirmation, I began to experience the presence and the power of the Angels.

Quickly, my secret desire for awareness and knowledge became transparent. I was no longer afraid of what people might think or say.

I began to trust my own judgement. I realised that I underestimated the gift God had bestowed upon me and I embraced the reawakening to the trust and belief that Angels really do exist. The idea of Angels and what they could do for me, for you, for everyone, immersed my being for some time.

My negative thinking became challenged. In my basic confused state I began to try to call upon the Angels; but at first, it was hard work.

I persevered, I didn't let go and believed that I was travelling along on a good path, with a spiritual quest to be conquered, a spiritual thirst to be satisfied. With practice and fortitude I began to experience the actions and the real presence of something or someone helping me.

Transference of mindset allowed me to enter into the profound world of God where I encountered not one Angel, but an army of Angels who empowered me to have courage to believe in what I had found, and to act accordingly. This had awakened the inner child; I reawakened the awareness and the profound belief that my childhood Guardian Angel was still with me, and was just waiting for me to call upon them in my time of need. This experience allowed me to unroll the reel of film which had captured my earlier phases of life and living.

Secretly, I thought: *'I wish I had realised this earlier'*, and laughed as I thought, *'My Angel would have been exhausted trying to satisfy my need for physical, psychological and spiritual wholeness'*.

Call upon your Angels. They cannot act alone; let them help you when you are in need. Never ever hesitate, your Angel really cares!

Affirmation

Truth be told, I suppose I needed affirmation that it was all right to have such an interest in cosmic spiritual beings and their impact on health and wholeness of self. Their eventual impact changed my thinking and impacted favourably upon my spiritual development.

We all search for something, we all need something. The reality is that frequently we are not sure what it is that we want, or, what we think we want! Indeed, it may be fair to suggest that it's not what we want that we have difficulty with, but to identify what it is, or what we *need* rather than want! As Jesus frequently asked *'What is it you want of me? What is it than I can do for you?'* We are invited to ask for that which we desire; it is not a sign of weakness, but, rather a sign of strength to identify the need for support and the courage to ask for help. When we love someone, we trust them; there are no barriers, no problem in asking for help. So too, when we realise the unconditional love God has for us, we cannot be afraid.

Sometimes, it is, difficult to understand or access answers to our quests but it is healthy to ask, to wait and to believe. We have to make every effort to identify with the pursuit for wholeness of self. Frequently, the experience of joy is attainable when we learn to trust and believe that

God has given each of us the gift of *'free will'* to seek and to understand; to gain confidence in self.

Yes!

We may fall, and we may stumble, but the gift of true faith will cushion us from the adversaries confronting us from time to time. Indeed, the answers to our requests may very well not be what we want, or what we expect: yet, with trust and belief, all things will be revealed. This will occur when the time is right, and what is the optimum for one's highest good, at that moment!

Within many gatherings the concept of *'Angels'*; the virtual reality of *'Angels'* and the submission to accepting that such a powerful force can influence life and living, it is quite exciting and this continues to draw attention from a growing audience of like-minded people.

Initially, the whole idea of Angelology seemed a little bit unsafe; it didn't seem right somehow; it didn't seem to warrant time and energy. I struggled whether to let myself suppose that it was reasonable to believe that Angels do exist, that Angels do enhance our wellbeing and that Angels do affect our spiritual growth or that the concept was a contemporary myth. Thus, the idea challenged me to further understand and to have the courage of my convictions.

Confidence

Occasionally, I meet and have met people who react in a way similar to the way in which I used to do myself: I lacked confidence and spent time in prayer seeking guidance before I developed a healthy belief in Angels. My insecurity was reflected when the topic surrounding the idea of Angels was discussed: I reacted, with an arrogant smirk of distain or a laugh covering up my real desire to know more about Angels. It is strange how other people influence or condition us. We have a responsibility to serve ourselves the best on the menu which provides the best possible diet to achieve wholeness of self.

Mary P worked all her life from the age of fifteen years. Her work was her life. Now in her late fifties Mary P faced an alien world where she just didn't seem to fit into anything. After being made redundant Mary P felt lost, desperate and became quite depressed. Mary P said: *'Despite enrolling and trying to participate in courses, I just couldn't. I just felt I had nothing to give, I had nothing to live for; my world was worthless, that is, until I met Hannah. I was going along the High Street in Haverhill, when out of the blue a woman approached me and gave me a leaflet: a glossy white sheet of paper with a printed invitation to join a creative writing course. Without even looking at its contents, I pushed the leaflet into my bag. A few days later while searching my bag for something, I came across the leaflet and opened it out and read it. 'That's not for me' I told myself.*

I convinced myself, but it was as if I could hear a voice saying 'Go on, why not'. Something seemed to tell me to read it again. I did. 'Hmmm! Maybe I will give this a go' I thought. Since then Mary P found a new life, a new circle of friends and a great sense of inner peace. Mary P acknowledged the quiet nudging of her Angel in a time of restlessness and need of direction.

Yes!

I was there too; life and living forced me to seek self help and inner healing. I too struggled to forge the relationship between the mystical nature of the Angels and the collective response of Society, Culture, the Church and their traditional practices. Likewise, Kelly, a young single mother was struggling to feel the presence of love, of hope and of faith shared her story filled with despair and hopelessness. She had been living in a place embodied in a sense of profound fear, as a result of harassment and bullying for a few years. Kelly clung like a leech to the belief of the Angels. She almost willed them to appear.

Kelly's deadened senses became alive; her spirit could see, hear, taste, smell and touch the essence of life again. The fear and the anxieties which gnawed at her through the period of poor treatment, gave way to a new wellbeing of self. The world of fear disappeared and Kelly grasped the opportunity to live with the renewed belief of God's love for her.

Then and since then, Kelly has and continues to experience the presence of the unseen and unheard spiritual beings who serve to please.

The notion that help can be achieved without any degree of hard work seems too ludicrous to understand.

But just like Kelly when we open ourselves to the belief that God wants to help us, yes, even those who are marginalised within society, those who feel they are not worthy, those who waver from side to side along the path of life, the best possible good for each of us is realised. Frequently, we may just be too busy or too annoyed to observe the changes which occur.

Through my own journey of life, many times, feathers fell upon my path but I hadn't really taken any heed, I didn't even notice them until through my search into the notion of Angels and their existence. When I associated the feather as a symbol of my Angel, I really embraced the concept with love. The simple presence of a feather was something that gave me affirmation. Little things became important, my confidence grew and I relished the experience of seeing feathers; (it seemed coincidental at first as my initial reaction was to check if there were birds or bird's nests nearby). Yet, I have frequently found a feather in the most unlikely places or situations.

Parking Angels can help when one needs a car parking space. I call upon my Angels when I need a parking space and this simple act of my Angel is of great value especially when only making a brief visit, to drop someone or something off, run into the Post Office or in town on business. Before leaving the house I ask the Angels, '*go ahead of me to get me a parking space*'; this always works, either I get there and there is a vacant space or another driver is just pulling out!

Through my journey into my search to know and believe in Angels, I have met the most beautiful spirited people, many who have made a positive imprint upon my life. I have accessed self-help therapists grounded in the Spirit of God.

I have escaped a number of near tragedies; fought numerous episodes of ill health, and have had the tremendous pleasure of being taken into the tunnel of heavenly light and feeling the majestic powers associated with *'out of body'* experiences.

I have called and continue to call upon the Angels frequently. In order to truly believe, I had to unlearn old beliefs and practices. Disposal of the old ways of thinking had to occur to allow me to accept and appreciate my life's mission. Such opened my mind and alerted me to taking a greater responsibility for myself. This demanded a new approach, a sense of belief alongside a renewed energy, into doing my utmost to achieve wholeness of self. I believe that the Angels bring that which is for my highest good; it is my desire to respond in kind to those around me.

In life and living, it is my desire to do my best to support those whom I love and those who care for me. My life is not a one way experience; it is a journey of various paths and avenues in which I continue to be open to what God wants of me; just as I want of Him. It is a two way process.

My ultimate aim is to *'love as I am loved; to serve as I am served; to hear as I have heard; to see as I have seen, and to reflect the Spirit of God which lives within me onto those whom I encounter.'*

Therefore, it is with great belief in Angels, in the healing power of the Angels and the gifts of Angels given to me by God, that, I share some understanding of what has become a profound and transformed attitude to that which I could not see; that which I could not perceive as possible and that which seemed somewhat crazy when I first began to try to accept that *'Angels'* do exist.

The revelation that my soul could be healed with the help of God's messengers *'unseen and unheard'*, excited me and such continues to stimulate me. Challenging times paved the way ahead; taking into consideration that Church and Church teachings focused on the mystery of Christ. This concept led me to reflect not only on the mystery of Christ but on the mystery of the Heavenly Kingdom, the eternal paradise which we strive to enter in time. This mystery of heaven, where a network of spiritual beings are ready to nurture the *'soul'* was indeed a challenge.

This led to the need to recognise that which belies and stunts spiritual growth and to become aware of the dimensions and realms from which *'Angels'* are borne.

Initially, the interest I had in relation to the Angels was based on wanting a wee bit of that which I was hearing others talk about. It was strange but there was something drawing my interest to this new dimension of thought. At the start of this journey I realised that many people were timid in their appraisal, even sceptical, but, I believed that it was worth examining. I guess I was just intrigued and wanted to understand, why the growing interest in Angels was creating such a stir? In time, I realised that to understand and appreciate the gift of the Angels and the acceptance of their existence, I was challenged to appreciate the mystery of Christ and the Angelic realm, and how they serve to help us whom God has created. Hand in hand, God and His messengers endeavour to help and support us.

How many times have we said or have heard people say *'There was definitely someone looking after me today, or I usually go to a particular place on the same day and time every week but was delayed which saved me from something potentially destructive or meeting someone with a negative aura.*

Sometimes it's only when we reflect that we can perceive that somewhere, somehow, we were protected by a power that we cannot fully begin to explain. In time we begin to recognize that something extraordinary, something majestic occurred. The awesome power of that which cannot be seen or heard, is too overwhelming to put into words; truly meaningful, heart filled words! So the invitation challenges one to be brave and courageous while journeying into the path of the unknown, where God waits to enlighten and empower spiritual development.

So you are asked to consider that Angels come when you call them. Angels do respond, just call!

Yes, they do—do they?

The invitation to call upon the Angels is for all!

Angels

There is a great awareness and interest today with regards to a conscious acceptance that there are some experiences and happenings which we just cannot explain. There is undoubtedly something mysterious which challenges a hunger to learn and feed the fundamental quest in relation to Angels. In an attempt to revitalise, rebuild and restore wholeness of self it is important to realise that ultimate well-being cannot be achieved without recognising and consequently addressing the need for help. Identifying the area of need is the first step on a diverse journey to complete well-being.

It seems that much attention has been given over recent years to two main facets of self, i.e. the physical and psychological dimensions of self. These two areas of self have gleaned support in which alternative and complementary approaches together with traditional medicine have served to help to nourish and benefit self development.

However, one facet of self has been somewhat neglected. The welfare of the soul has not really been recognised as an equally important part of self in need of support and development. Yet, just like anything, if any part of the whole is not functioning then the ultimate and optimum performance is less likely to be realised: e.g. if the inner mechanisms of a clock are not working in

Kate O'Kane

unison, it cannot achieve its best, irrespective of its outer appearance. Despite the conventional and somewhat traditional approach to spiritual well–being, Church rituals and devotions have been challenged: it's not enough to offer services; people need more, demand more; those who are searching need answers, and affirmation to help them fully appreciate the mystery of life. So the encouragement of spiritual development is to be encouraged with guidance and support.

Hence, the modern day challenge to understand the phenomenon of Angels, their existence, their power and their affect in relation to self help, is exciting despite hidden fears of opening up to something new! In the midst of sickness, death, loss, discord and more, the need for help is vital but sometimes it is a great challenge to realise that it is not weak to ask, it is actually a sign of great personal strength.

Is there the chance that we fear the reactions of others; are we influenced by others to the extent that we starve our desire to glean information about the concept of healing of self through the power of the Angels? The fundamental notion that we can avail of some sort of healing energy from God is one thing, but, the notion that an *'unseen and unheard'* spiritual being can bring about a sense of well–being is a difficult phenomenon for many people to consider.

Therefore, it is a challenge to be courageous enough to obtain, sustain and maintain a healthy interest in that which cannot be seen, that which cannot be explained but that which brings comfort and strength. Over the past number of years for some people the ideology surrounding the concept of *'Angels'* may have appeared to be a ludicrous and almost crazy supposition which has sustained a level of negative and cautious deliberation. So often, people have said to me: *"Angels! Surely you don't believe in Angels? You might as well believe in fairies!"*

Yet, somewhere, somehow there were as many people with a real desire to believe that Angels do exist. Sourcing relevant information was difficult. There was much more to read than one could have envisaged. Contemplation, meditation, Lectio Divina strengthened my resolve. Various journeys opened up new approaches and methods to my search for information. When people meet those with an interest in Angels, there is an immediate bond. Maggie told me *"It was great to hear you mention Angels. I have had an interest in Angels but was scared to say to anyone. I thought people would think I was crazy. I have read books; I have an Angel on my bedside table. But, I want to really believe and not have a fear to share my views"*.

While on various travels I have frequently met people who share this interest, I have had occasions where my liberal belief of Angels has been acknowledged. When in South Dakota with a troupe of Irish dancers, two young girls presented me with a copy of Native American Spirituality in which Beatrice Weasel Bear points out to us that *"The four Angels in the four directions are waiting"*.

Albeit a slow, cautious consideration, the idea of spiritual beings, *'Angels'* has grown in awareness, acceptance and appreciation. In modern society, people are more open to seeking help, more open to recognising personal responsibility and accountability for self development and growth. People are more aware and more prepared to seek help through the use of technology, and alternative and complementary therapies, resources available to all. The awareness, acceptance and appreciation of Angels, reveal the spiritual healing which enhance the spirit within!

Yet, sometimes we don't readily admit our inner quest or acknowledge the presence of an Angel.

When Jean went to visit with friends in South Dakota, her spirit was reawakened when she and Anne travelled via Rapid City on their way to the Black Hills. Along the way the two ladies got into a conversation about Angels. *"Do you believe in Angels?"* Anne asked Jean. Hesitantly, Jean replied *"You know what . . . I think I do, with that a deer ran out from the tall tree which lined the wide twisting road; the deer startled Anne who jammed on the brakes immediately. Suddenly the deer stopped and stood bold and strong in front of the car. There was something so striking and wonderful about the animal, sparkling eyes that seem to shine and a radiance of light floating around the car. Anne decided to wait patiently in her usual calm manner until the animal left. The deer danced and performed in a playful manner as it made its way into the dense woodland at the other side of the road. 'What about that then? I wasn't expecting that, were you? Anne said with a glint of mischief in her smile'"*. As Jean paused, I seemed to sense what she was going to tell me as she took up the story again: *"Before we moved on, Anne decided we should put the snow chains on, as the road was rather slippery. The day light was beginning to drop and the stark white tinted trees began to shed some Angel dust as the wind tugged the snow dressed trees. As we moved off down the broad road past log cabins on either side towards Rapid City, a gigantic lorry came at great speed around the bend before us and seemed to be coming directly towards us!*

We believed that was it! I just put my head into my hands and said God protect us. The lorry skimmed passed us. Screeching and whining, the brakes of the lorry struggled. As if in slow motion, the lorry veered towards the crash bars and just missed hitting Anne's car!

The slippery road surface caused the car to skid a little. After being jolted about, we both sat gob-smacked. We couldn't speak. Anne looked at me. I looked at her. Then Anne said 'Well now do you believe in Angels?' Yes, I do, I replied without hesitation. If the deer hadn't appeared and delayed us as it did, and, we hadn't stopped to put on the snow chains, the story would possibly have been very different. The eyes of deer were so beautiful, so bright and calming I have absolutely no doubt that we were saved by an Angel that day".

Jean's testimony reveals the affirmative growth of attitude and belief when we encounter such an experience. Sometimes we need to be confronted by something extraordinary in order to believe and that is quite normal, such is a common trait and is effectually positive.

We have the tools at our disposal. There is a vast amount of literature and resources available to everyone who seeks to help themselves to a better and fuller life. There is a wealth of knowledge readily available within the Bible. There are many *'Light workers'*, those who fully embrace the power of God's Messengers and who seek to serve those in need. God wishes us to participate in making this world a better and safer and more loving place.

Moving outside the norm, the acceptance and consideration of self-help is achieved with an open and balanced approach, in which, the importance of conventional medicine is not isolated, but, rather included when choosing an appropriate method to working on a programme towards obtaining and sustaining wholeness of self. Through various advertising, self-help groups and government focus on health matters, a greater awareness and recognition towards the concept of self-help is highlighted and greatly encouraged.

Emphasis has been placed upon the invitation to individuals to appreciate and accept the responsibility to achieving and enjoying a positive sense of wellbeing. For some time, the modern approach to ultimate well-being focused mainly on the physical and psychological needs of self. Beauty and personal care have been the predominant means towards restoring, repairing and revitalising the physical self and self image. Therefore, the outer shell has been well catered for; cosmetics in various forms are readily available and dietary programmes are encouraged.

Psychological health, irrational thought, and emotional health also began to receive a lot of awareness and attention; many therapies including reflexology, acupuncture and massage were recognised and accepted as being worthy contributors to achieving ultimate well-being. So, there are choices available for anyone seeking help. These various therapies could either be used alongside traditional or conventional medicine and/or used alone. We are all blessed with the gift of *'free will'*. Such has been encouraged. Choice has become an important factor in relation to the successful quest for individual wellness.

However, it is important to realise that the ego while quite fragile can prove to be problematic. Indeed, the ego can steer us away from that which we need, for some it's easy to believe we don't need help, we can do it alone. This reflects how God fits or maybe doesn't fit within the lives of some people.

Teresa, a gifted energy therapist shared her description of the ego when she said *"I refer to the ego as 'easing God out'*.

In recent times, people are opting to use alterative and/or complementary approaches; employing a mix of the *'new and the old'* means focusing on attaining good health. However, what is clear is that outside of Church the soul didn't seem to be deemed worthy of some sort of support and/or help. Indeed, maybe many people did not appreciate the need to look at what their perception of need, means to them. It's easy to believe that surely the spiritual dimension and consequential growth of the spiritual self were the remit of the institutional Church. It may be the case that there was a reluctance to acknowledge that there was a substantial spiritual void or emptiness and that it is a personal choice to seek that which is for one's highest good. Such a concept required not only a new approach but an acceptance for new thought and understanding. Traditionally, it was perceived by many that the Church seemed to own the sole responsibility to provide and prescribe some form of medicine for the soul.

Ironically, many people in contemporary society have turned away from Church for various reasons, directly or indirectly: for some they believe such to be right, for some it may be simply a means of *'pointing the finger at'* or placing the blame onto to something or someone else because of their own personal inadequacies to believe. More recently through various forms of self exploration and education we have begun to *'take up the mantle'* so to speak, and realise that everyone has a personal journey paved with experiences and encounters which reflect daily life and living.

Only in more recent times has it become more apparent and accepted that the soul is an important and integral part of the wholeness of a person, and people have awakened to the idea that they too have to work to achieve that which is for one's best. It is suggested that spiritual healing can happen, yet, it may not have received a great deal of acknowledgement until quite recently. However, the concept has provoked much thought and continues to gain a profound sense of consciousness.

The healing power of the Angels has become an exciting phenomenon embraced by people of all faith traditions. The beautiful image and the idea that a heavenly presence accompanies us and the belief that Angels do exist, has provided, a greater sense of belonging and acceptance of God and God's unconditional love for each of us. The more we call upon the Angels, the more their energy becomes an apparent presence. The more we call upon the Angels, the more grace we receive; the more we receive the more we believe. The more grace we receive, the greater the ability to embrace and hold firm to the concept that we are people worthy of God's love, support and guidance.

Even in the most bizarre happenings God's protectors are ready to respond to our call as Terry exclaimed with an air of excitement: *"I was about to cross the road at the traffic lights, ye know, down there near the 'Holy Shop'. Well as always, even though the lights may change to green, before moving off the path, I look up and down the road for traffic. There definitely was no sign of any traffic. When I was about half way across the road a small red car appeared out of nowhere. I couldn't believe my eyes"*, Terry said as she grabbed my arm and continued. *"I started to run but tripped and the sweat was lashing off me. In my sheer panic I didn't believe that I could be saved. I huddled into myself and called on my Angels, 'please help me Michael' I said and at that instant the car stopped.*

I was lying within an inch of the vehicle and just lay there in sheer and utter relief. People gathered around me and one person asked me if they could contact Michael for me but I looked up at her and explained that Michael was my Archangel who is always there to help me. As I got up I was relieved that there was nothing hurt, not even my pride. I know if it wasn't for my belief in the

Angels I would have been hit at least. So I for one can safely say that Angels really do exist".

I share Terry's profound belief in Angels.

I can freely identify with the belief of the existence of the Angels. I have experienced the healing power of the Angels and my inner peace has become so powerful, that I can face any storm with the belief that God in his merciful loving kindness will hear my prayer and provide that which is for my highest good.

In order to embrace the healing power of the Angels, the existence of the Angels and the Ascended Masters i.e. great spiritual teachers, leaders or healers who have walked upon the Earth: Jesus, Mary and all the Saints. Many Saints have openly told of their love for and their relationships with the Angels, such as St. Pio of Pietrelcina; St. Fustina, John Paul II, St. Therese of the Child Jesus (the Little Flower), St. John of God and St. Francis of Assisi. It is important to explore the associated elements of awareness and appreciation of God's Heavenly guides, their purpose and their usefulness. The Angels, the Archangels and the Ascended Masters all play powerful roles in which they work to bring God's love in abundance to each of His creation.

Therefore, many questions easily came to mind seeking answers and understanding regarding Angels, their role, their existence and the theological stance in relation to this growing interest in Angelology.

Fundamental questions which may arise:

Do Angels exist?
If they do—what are Angels?
What are Archangels?
What is the sole purpose of an Angel?
How can we access the healing power of the Angels?
Are signs and symbols indicators of spiritual energies?
How do we know when Angels are near?
Does everyone have one Angel and/or more?
How many times do we hear people refer to someone as *'a wee Angel'* or *'There was definitely someone looking after me!'*?
Have you ever felt as if there was someone near you even though you are alone? Or in the darkness a light appears!
Are we aware of the importance of the Angels in relation to Scripture?
Can we imagine Christian living without the assistance of God's Messengers? Messengers of healing, protection and communication!

As Jesus said to the blind man even though he knew the man couldn't see, *"What is it that I can do for you?"* What a question to ask, surely Jesus could see the man was blind. Therefore, in this Jesus reminds us that while he knows our needs and our desires, it is up to us to ask. We have the *'free will, the choice'*, to ask for help. God cannot and must not be just taken for granted. *'Ask and you shall receive; seek and you will find; knock and the door shall be opened unto you!' Ask God for the help, support and protection needed even though He is aware of our every need. Don't be afraid to ask. Be humble knowing God knows your needs and desires.*
Yes!

God knows our needs and desires, so call the Angels without delay.

As in contemplation, meditation, and Lectio Divina, we are invited to rest, to listen and to allow change to occur. In silence the Lord and His Angels speak words of wisdom.

In the darkness, we embrace the light.

Even a tiny glimmer of light is a sign of Hope.

A tiny particle of Hope creates Love.

It is of importance that the views of those who are sceptical to the notion of Angels are treated with respect. No-one has the right to force their views onto others; everyone has a voice, an opinion which they have the right to express as they possess the great gift of *'free will'*. But there is an increased belief that Angels exist. When Angels are present, pause, and be aware of the energetic force grounded in serenity and peace within your space.

Together a mix of Hope and Love create Faith. When any of these three vital elements: Hope, Love and Faith are weakened, the physical, psychological and spiritual aspects of self may become dis-eased. When disease has taken hold and manifests itself within, take heed, and treat it with due care and attention. Just as a tumour must be removed for the greater good of the whole; so too, when that which is diseased is recognised and treated, it is more likely to be healed. It is better to have less for the greater good of the whole.

We need something to hold on to in our time of need.

Therefore, we must ask God for help.

Call upon the Angels;

We must trust them to do and to bring about that which is for our highest good!

And remember that they, the Angels, cannot act without an invitation!

Angels come in various forms, human or otherwise. There are Angels assigned to the care of persons, animals, nature and more.

To enable Angels to respond, it is good to explore the concept of Angels. In order to appreciate and trust in the concept of Angels be at ease and appreciate the gift bestowed. Open to the Angels.

What are Angels?

The word Angel comes from the Greek word 'Angelos,' meaning messenger. An Angel is therefore one who can act as a messenger or an agent of God. The role of a Guardian Angel is to guide us in our thoughts, words and deeds and to preserve us from evil. Angels are ministering spirits who serve to bring about that which is for our highest good. Holy angels work for the glorification of God and the sanctification of souls. In the Old Testament, the Hebrew for *'Angel'* is Malak which also means messenger. St. Thomas Aquinas referred to Angels as spiritual beings which transcend all religions, philosophies and creeds. He suggested that *'Angels have no religion as we know it. Their existence precedes every religious system that ever existed on earth . . .'*. Many of us realise the concept of Angels as spiritual beings that assist and guard us, and this may be a challenge for others.

A feather, bright and light; the presence or wafts of warm air which cannot be explained are symbolic in relation to the awareness and the existence of Angels.

In lay terms we all can identify with, questions that emerge without effort in relation to the concept of *'Angels'*. An understanding and acceptance of Angels cannot be achieved without due consideration and questioning.

'So, what are Angels?' I hear you say!

'Angels are the Messengers of God'.

Angels are God's aides who wish to accompany us through life and living.

Angels are heavenly beings whose ultimate function is to assist us throughout our earthly journey. Angels are loving kind guides; their goal is to bring about peace, happiness, guidance and support towards inner peace and wholeness. Angels bring God's grace and trust to us: when relationships, health issues, careers, financial needs impact negatively upon our well-being.

The help and the guidance of the Angels is never-ending, there are no limitations to what the Angels can do for us. There is never anything too big or too small. Angels serve to protect and guard us from harm. Their objective is to generate perfect peace on earth as a consequence of spiritual healing brought about with the uplifting of one person at a time. It is difficult to perceive the concept that an unseen and unheard being can act and respond by bringing help and support in the time of need. With subsequent courage, trust and respectful patience the power of the Angels can bring about tremendous transformation of self.

When positive transformation occurs there is a ripple effect. When change is realised, everyone benefits. And, when we are confident as regards our awareness, acceptance and appreciation of the *'Angels'*, we can freely share our belief with others without any fear of contradiction.

As a result of Ruby's belief in the Angels, her daughter began to recognise signs and symbols associated with the presence of the Angels. Her mother in a quiet voice told me how her daughters attitude has changed: *"She told me she stops every time she finds a feather"*. Ruby continued excitedly: *"What's more, one day we decided to go to visit the grave where my wee grandson is buried. As we approached the gate there was a gentle warm breeze despite the stillness of the day. As I put my hand on the gate a feather fell upon my hand. As we approached the grave, two birds were singing as they sat upon the Teddy bear for Baby Peadar".* Looking convincingly at me, Ruby proudly declared *"I knew the Angels were there".*

Sometimes strange things happen which we cannot describe or understand: an incident, an occurrence, an encounter which is unexpected or unexplainable. Sometimes because of the bizarre nature of our experiences we may keep such experiences to ourselves with the fear that if we dare to share the story, people may think we're crazy. Not so, everyone has such experiences whether they share these or not. When you take time and remain calm, there will emerge a reason, an understanding and a meaning for such an occurrence.

Therefore, in simple terms

'What are Angels?'

What are Angels?
            Spirits unseen, unheard.
                  Spirits!

What are Spirits?
            Presence unseen, unheard.
                  Presence!

What is Presence?
            Serenity unseen, unheard.
                  Serenity!

What is Serenity?
            Peacefulness unseen, unheard.
                  Peacefulness!

What is Peacefulness?
            Serenity unseen, unheard.
                  Presence unseen, unheard.

                      Spirits unseen, unheard.
                Angels unseen, unheard!

Spirit presence brings serenity and peacefulness in unseen, unheard Angelic form—Angels!'

Awareness, Acceptance and Appreciation of the Angels

Therefore, there has been a growing Awareness, Acceptance and Appreciation which enables a profound sense of Acknowledgement to the validity and worth of various therapies; these have begun to be more readily embraced as valuable methods and tools to achieving and sustaining a healthier state of being.

As a consequence of my personal journey and work with the Angels this paradigm has emerged as the concept of the *'Angels'* is explored. This model the *'3 A's'* explores the Awareness, Acceptance and Appreciation of the concept of Angels and leads to the Acknowledgement of the existence and activity of such spiritual beings. The *'3 A's'* are powerfully inclusive factors in relation to the way forward, especially, in relation to Angelology, considering that for generations the emotions and spiritual needs of individual souls had been unintentionally neglected.

Stress, anger, hurt, fear, loneliness, and isolation are some examples of emotions we all experience from time to time. Yet when these are neglected, a manifestation of a physical or psychological nature will inevitably emerge. Angels watch as we struggle and eagerly await our call. Can we even begin to imagine what it must be like as

Angels are aware of our needs, yet, are helpless without an invitation to serve?

Quite often we don't even know what is wrong, why we feel the way we do or how to explain what is going on. Sometimes it is very difficult to identify our needs. The emotional side of our being is sensitive and responsive to the external and internal mechanisms of our bodies. What happens to our bodies whether physically or psychologically affects our inner being. When the emotions are distorted and confusion emerges, our spiritual capacity to grow becomes depleted, fragile and lethargic. An inner haemorrhage may occur, anaemia brings forth apathy, fear and withdrawal which gives way to a dull and gloomy world.

When this happens, it is important to realise that the soul, the spiritual side of self, is in need of help. So just as the physical and psychological wellbeing are important and require care and due attention, so too, is the wellbeing of the spirit. If one part of self is hurt or broken, so too, the other parts of self are affected. As a perfect specimen of fruit in its ripe condition looks good, and in time the outer skin is bruised, it is not possible to envisage the inner damage within until the skin is peeled back.

So too there is a real tendency to imagine that which looks good on the outside reflects the interior. Yet, the inner damage to mind, body and soul can be greatly in need. To attain the ultimate sense of wellbeing it is imperative that we remember to acknowledge the need to achieve not only a wholeness of self but also a sustainable balance of body, mind and soul.

Hence, the belief and the actions of the Angels in our daily life and living provide an important and meaningful comfort and support to well-being and true peace. When we let the Angels into our daily life and living, we experience an awareness of the gift they bring to us from God. Then we appreciate and accept their presence and acknowledge the power of the Angels. The Angels are powerful envoys who work to bring about the best for each of us, that which is for our highest good. The Angels wait and respond when we call.

The Angels are happiest when we receive God's love in abundance. Angels are at our service. They are God's messengers: we do not worship them but it is important to thank them for their unfailing help. We have a responsibility to make use of and to call upon the Angels who wish only to serve.

Have you ever tried to call upon 'Parking Angels' when you need a space to park?

Have you ever wanted some sort of a sign or an affirmation that Angels exist?

Do you stop when a feather falls upon your path?

Do you question the sweet fragrance in a place when there is nothing evident?

Or have you ever had a thought or a quiet sense that something just doesn't seem right?

Or have you had a feeling that there is someone nearby when it is physically impossible?

Have you felt that warm waft of air pass by? You experience a soft tender breeze around you; it's so comforting that you just know that all is well.

Have you heard the Angels whisper or a voice speak to you in the silence?

Have you experienced hearing your name being called when there's no-one around?

Sometimes you may feel a presence or just get a feeling that something is right or not right for you. Such are affirmations that the Angels are present.

Frequently, we may be reluctant to express our beliefs. The influences of others may allow us to be afraid of what others may think. So often we give other people the power to suppress our thoughts, our feelings and/or our actions.

Stop!

We are given the gift of *'free choice'*? As Christians we are given many tools to assist us through the journey of life and living. Within the Scriptures, within the Liturgies of Church services, in the availability of the Sacraments and in the 'Eucharist': (in the *'eating and drinking'* of the body and blood of the one who came so we could be saved, the real presence of God), there is a wealth of spiritual support readily available. *'Christianity is fundamentally based on belief. Belief is the fundamental basis of Christianity'.* This doctrine reflects the profound wealth of support available to each of us. Spiritual nourishment is vital.

The Angels play a vital role in providing the food of life; the ingredients of love, hope and faith when liberally blended together generate an amazing creation. There are no conditions. This food is for all. Just call and you will be fed.

Yeah! Yeah! I hear you say . . . . but be assured this does work. These Messengers of God are employed to assist us earthly beings through the journey of life and living.

'Be not afraid' is so often versed. So listen! Hear the words. Believe the words. Live the words.

Trust!

Call and the Angels will act with immediacy and deep love to serve.

When you believe, embrace and welcome the Angels, you will recognise your Angel at work! And when you experience the joy and the love of God you will realise the existence of the Angels. This may appear surreal, fantastic and dreamlike but be reassured that with Angels within and around you, nothing and no-one, will extinguish the spiritual fire that is lit within you. As the soul awakens to new life, the inner healing will sustain and enhance the spirit and in time this powerful healing will affect the body, mind and soul to become fully integrated and well.

The essence of life and living is enhanced; a well-balanced being can overcome adversaries. Let the wholeness of self be renewed. Reach out and embrace the Angels who wait to serve.

The image of an Angel is personal; for some people, an Angel may have a divine appearance with the most beautiful feathered wings ever envisaged; a human being radiating love and happiness, or a faceless non-gender figure. Either way, the important thing to remember is that the Angel is the gift God has given: the unseen, unheard being of the heavenly sphere who will guide and protect; who will respond to our call and who will endeavour to do all within its power to bring about that which is ultimately for our highest good.

The Angel is the one whom God has sent to help us achieve love, happiness and peace while on this planet. We are not sent here to suffer, we are sent here to do the best we can with the time and the tools available to us. God has given us all the gift of *'free-will'*; it is our personal choice to believe, to call and to appreciate what God has designed to be our spiritual aides. In embracing and accepting the gift of the Angels, the healing power of the Angels and the love of God brought about by the Angels, it is also important to note and understand *'Angels'*: their function and role in bringing about ultimate joy, love and peace into our hearts which in turn will benefit all. This will help to make the world a much better place for everyone and everything.

Therefore, on occasions an opportunity will help us focus on the acknowledgement to be aware that Angels do exist; accept their contribution to humanity and appreciate the activity of God's messengers who serve to please. In so doing we will experience the work of the Angels and how we too work with the Angels.

Linda shared this story with me a few years ago. I was so intrigued that I have never forgotten how she believed her friend Connie exemplified working with her Angel: *'I was walking home from the town late one December night. It was dry. It was cold. The frosty sky was bright. There wasn't a sound. I was feeling lonely and nervous and eventually was feeling scared as I passed by the graveyard wall. In the silence I heard footsteps behind me. I began to run and as I did, so too did the footsteps behind me.*

I was breathless as the sound of the footsteps began to grow in tandem with mine! I prayed into myself: Angels where are you? Oh? God protect me! Suddenly I could see a figure approaching me. From out of nowhere Connie appeared. I was so glad to see her. I couldn't even speak, I was so relieved. When I told her of my experience she laughed. "Sure there's not a being about", she chuckled. "Maybe it was your imagination" she continued. Initially I was really annoyed with her but later I could understand that it could very well have been my imagination. Either way I realised that my prayer was answered. Connie was used by the Angels to save me from a frightening and weird experience".

As with Linda's experience which may seem insignificant to someone else, the fact remains that somewhere within the midst of any level of uncertainty, the inner self is fragile; the soul is tender and in need of affirmation and support. So embrace the force of the Angelic realm and live. It is unfair to minimise anyone's experience. Every human being is unique and every individual experience is very different. It is important to *'Embrace this Angelic form who comes . . .'.*

Embrace this Angelic form who comes

An easy presence hangs around,
although it's busy, there's not a sound,
A warmth, calmness falls with ease,
for those in need, we try to please!
The one who calls in silent tone,
draped in fear, sad, alone.

An Angel sent from God above
hovers close as the peaceful dove.
Encase this Angelic form who comes
to ease life's dreary storm.
'A messenger from God' is here,
to cradle you and avert your fear.

An easy presence hangs around
amidst the toil, there is no sound.
God heard a call and an Angel sent
to the one now quiet and serene.
A warmth, a calmness falls with ease
to the one in need, whom God will please.

Encase this Angelic form that comes
to ease life's dreary storm:
'A messenger from God' is here,
to cradle you, and avert your fear.

The challenge is there for each of us, to open our hearts and embrace the goodness and love of the *'Angels'*. It is important to recognise the need for help; to embrace the confidence to do what is necessary to fulfil the needs for wellbeing and to have the courage to call upon the Angels for their help and support. The soul yearns to be refreshed, restored and renewed. The spiritual journey continues to grow with the assistance and support of the Angelic realm, as the Angels work to bring about that which is for our highest good!

So what do Angels do?

What kind of work do Angels do?

Why do Angels wait?

Their patience is timeless. Angels will respond, just believe. God is full of love for each and every one of us! Sometimes the work of the Angels may be experienced in the most unlikely form; that which we cannot understand, that which we cannot see, that which we cannot comprehend. A fellow human being, a friend or an unexpected encounter may well show the work of the Angels.

By and large, when the **3 A's** are realized, we become aware of the Angels, what they represent, what they do and how they work: when we become fully aware we begin to accept that Angels exist, work and serve we whom God has created: when we accept we learn to appreciate the great gift God has bestowed upon us. To be aware, to accept and to appreciate the concept of Angels, such eventually gives way to a greater belief which leads to a profound acknowledgement of the ministering spirits of God.

The work of the Angels

For most people there comes a time in one's life when the day-to-day routines and hassles of life become problematic. The physical, psychological and spiritual depletion of self incurs periods of ill health, depression, emptiness, dryness and loss.

As contemporary society has tentatively grasped the concept of self-empowerment and healing, it is vital that all elements of well-being are incorporated in endeavouring to replenish the flailing self. Angels will instantly attend to your request, indeed it is suggested that the Archangels can attend to more than one request at a time. Just think *'Angel'*, or say *'Angel'* and you will instantly know that your Angel is with you.

As Angels have no gender appropriated to them, it is not surprising that sometimes we do not envisage an image in which we can determine whether the Angel is male or female. So don't be put off, continue to allow God to send to you that which is for your highest good. The form is not important, yet, symbols and signs often arise. It is at this point that we become alert to the awareness, acceptance and appreciation of the Angelic form: we begin to recognise the effects of a feather, a breeze, a vision or the unexpected visit or person that appears in time of need.

Within the Angelic realm of Heaven, a number of Angels wait with great joy and quiet excitement to fulfil their duty to help human beings in need. The power of the Angelic Realm is one that is unseen and unheard, which is made up of Angels, Archangels representative of the presence of God, the heavenly sensitive and dynamic power of spiritual healing.

As anxiety, stress, fear, sadness, loneliness, and many other factors take centre stage in one's life there is an invaluable wealth of spiritual support waiting to be called upon. God readily responds and gives those who call for help, an awareness of the abundance of Angelic guides waiting to assist those in need.

Call upon the Angels and allow them to work for you. Angels are happiest when they are busy. There are still some people who find that concept hard to believe. However, when a person is at rock bottom, or lonely, depressed or weary with fear and angst about sickness, death and things we cannot control, it is at such times we need something to hold on to!

A young man shared this story with me while I was attending a Baptist Service in Mitchell, SD: *"It was a Friday, I will never forget. It was 3 o'clock. It was really dark. Physically dark! It was scary. It's still so hard to explain . . . I didn't know what was happening but I just knew it wasn't good. Faces of young people whom I knew who had died came flashing in front of me, one at a time. Each face looked so beautiful, so happy. It was as if they were willing me to join them.*

I cried out. I roared out: God where are you? Please help me. I was crying. I felt so alone and so afraid. I called out a number of times. Then the phone rang, it was my sister, if she had been with me I would have smothered her with hugs. She listened to me; she reassured me and distracted my attention away from the awful episode filled with fear. She asked me to trust in God; to feel the Angels presence and to rest my spirit".

Ever since then I always refer to my sister as my *'Angel'*. The experience somehow has helped me to believe and trust that there is a spiritual entity there waiting to help.

We are invited to trust, to believe and to accept and use all the tools that are available to help make life and living the best it can be.

And while Angels are assigned to each of us, we have the choice. Yes, God has given each of us the gift of *'free will'*, therefore, Angels cannot act, direct, guide or do anything without an invitation, except in very exceptional situations!

Have you ever experienced that moment when you decided not to go somewhere. You set out to go and met someone whom you thought was keeping you back or even making you anxious; maybe even dancing from foot to foot! Then you found out later that you were saved from some strange occurrence or potentially dreadful experience? And when you look back and think how it all unfolded, it is possible to notice the working of an unseen, unheard Angel.

It is important that we co-operate with the Angels. But, how do we co-operate with the Angels? Angels were created for the praise and service of God, their mission is to lead people to God. We must not praise or adore the Angels; we call upon the Angels and pray to the Angels as a means to seek God's support and help. It is however, important that we remember to thank God and the Angels for graces received.

When seeking wholeness of self, it is worth remembering the need to be aware of the cracks in need of repair. The Angels are eagerly waiting to help us achieve wholeness of self.

To invoke the Angels, all one needs to do is to say *'Angels'* or *'Angels please come to my aid'* and your Angel will respond. It's that simple.

Working with the Angels

It's only fair to suggest that if we call upon the Angels, we have a responsibility to work with them when and if such should arise! However, it takes time to become aware, accept and appreciate this miraculous phenomenon. With experience and belief it may become a partnership in which the Angels work for us and we work with them.

Mary-Anne, a lady from the Midwest shared this experience as we travelled from Minneapolis. She indicated that her Angel had directed her but she too had played a vital role: *"My little girl was in the hospital, her temperature was soaring . . . I felt helpless and gazed upon her little pale face. I called out 'Raphael' where are you?*

A nurse ran quickly in response to my call. She looked pensively at me and rested her hand on my shoulder. Who is Raphael? She asked. Can I ring him for you? She continued. . . . Looking up at her I quietly explained it was an Angel I was calling. 'It was the Archangel St. Raphael to whom I was calling'. To my amazement she confided that she too believed in Angels and instantly a bright shimmering emerald green light shone over my little girl. The light became immersed in vibrant colours as majestic as a rainbow around all of us. Together the nurse and I welcomed the presence of Raphael. Together we prayed as the powerful light spread like a blanket around us all. As the heat emerged it was evident that something extraordinary was happening. It was so peaceful, so beautiful, and just brilliant! As the light and the heat subsided my little girl stirred contentedly smiling towards us. There was no doubt that a great healing had occurred. Together, the nurse and I held my little girl's hands in a Trinitarian manner. As tears rolled down my cheeks we thanked Archangel Raphael for his help and spiritual support".

Mary-Anne's story epitomised the working partnership of Angels and humans in unison. Another example of working with Angels emerged while I was in Lourdes, France. My sister and I walked down towards the Grotto. As we approached the bridge, I could see an invalid man losing control of his wheelchair as he turned from the bridge. As the sacred place is to be treated with the utmost silence and respect, I could find myself wanting to call out . . . . *'Please help. Oh, God please help'*. It was difficult not to shout out but I called loudly within and ran to help the man in the wheelchair.

As the wheelchair ran uncontrollably onto the uneven ground towards the Grotto, I ran as fast as I could. I tried to indicate to other people nearer to him to help him. Just as I approached him the wheelchair fell over onto its side. *'It was like watching something happen in slow motion'*. It was as if I went into auto pilot, I reached for the man as he fell. Despite his fine physical appearance he was heavy to hold, but somehow, from somewhere, I got the strength to hold him until a passerby lifted the wheelchair up and together we struggled to get him back into the wheelchair. As I got the man settled and calmed him down, my sister caught up with us. The poor man was badly shaken. He smiled tenderly and thanked us saying, *"That as I was coming over the bridge I could feel the wheelchair go out of control and I called upon the Angels for help"*. Then he continued to say, *'There is no doubt my Angel heard my call and sent you to help me'*. I realised that it wasn't just a case of being in the right place at the right time; it was a case of being there to do the physical work of the Angels.

Sometimes, it's difficult to see the Angels at work. It's also difficult to recognise when you are working with the Angels. Sometimes, it's a long time before everything falls into place, before one can become aware, accept and appreciate the reasons why we do what we do!

Stephen had called on his Angel Guardian for help. He said, *'When I realised I was losing control of my wheelchair, I called to God. Help me! Help me! I shouted and as the wheels turned faster and faster. I asked, where are you God? As I descended the downward slope of the bridge I prayed like I never have prayed before despite all the pain and loss in my life'*. His Angel heard and quickly helped him and without thinking I was there beside him to lift him without any decision to be made. I was undoubtedly guided to assist this person in need. He was protected by the work of the Angels and saved from a possible tragedy. When it was all over, we turned towards the Grotto, relieved and in thanksgiving we huddled together; (Stephen, Mary and myself) and said a prayer of thanksgiving.

Arm in arm my sister and I left the Grotto and talked of the amazing thing we had just experienced and instantly recognised the work of the Angels. On the way up towards the hotel, the first shop we came upon had a window display of Angel statues which drew our attention. There they were: Archangels Michael, Raphael and Gabriel. Michael the Archangel in his fine armoured figure resembled the serene yet strong image of Stephen; it was almost a mirror image of the invalid man and the robust muscular figure which he bore. As we walked towards the upper bridge we reflected on the experience and rather excitedly hurried to share our story.

We made our way towards *'Marguerites'* where we shared the story with the shopkeeper who immediately gasped: she listened attentively before throwing her arms around me and saying, *'You are an Angel in disguise'*. She continued, *'God bless you. God sent you to help that poor man'*. Somewhere deep within I had a feeling that I had just met Michael the Archangel face-to-face.

Initially I felt drained, I was exhausted but later I felt a swell of energy I couldn't explain. The spiritual essence of my pilgrimage grew and the graces afforded to my sister and myself were awesome. On our return to the Grotto that evening we sat beyond the statues of *'Mary the Blessed Mother and St. Bernadette'* where together we recited the rosary for the man whom we had helped earlier. Every experience whether big or small, is spirit filled, if we only but take time to appreciate what is happening. Since that encounter and working with the Angels my confidence and belief that Angels do indeed exist has continued to grow.

Nothing is without reason. There is a purpose and a reason for all that happens. The people we meet awaken something within. The tasks which confront us challenge us to be patient, to believe and to trust. Even the love we give to our pets is an expression of God's deity. Angels assist all, even pets. As Laura explained: *"I have the most gentle and beautiful dog ever. She is called Patch, a name she brought with her because of the black patch over her left eye. One day when I was working in the garden I decided to stop and have a break. As I sat on the bench Patch decided to join me. She jumped up and her front leg got caught between the wooden slats. It's hard to explain this, but, somehow I didn't even panic. Patch trusted me. I manoeuvred her leg until I freed her and then I massaged her leg and prayed that she would be alright. Within seconds the swelling disappeared. After cuddling her for a brief moment I put Patch down and she just ran off, not a limp, nothing. There is no doubt that God helped this helpless little creature in my care".*

It is true, there are reasons for everything but often it is difficult to believe. There is a reason, there is a purpose, and there is a time to call upon the Angels. That is an individual choice; but the Angels are always waiting and ready to respond, to take our concerns to God!

There is a time for everything . . . . Ecclesiastes 3:1-8

All things come to those who wait.

God answers our prayers in His time.

When to call the Angels!

There is no right or wrong way or no right or wrong time in which to call for Angels to help. Calling upon the Angels is not a structured practice. It is something spontaneous. It is an individual quest. It is a personal choice based on belief and trust. Just as in the incident experienced by Stephen when he realised his wheelchair was uncontrollable, he instantly called upon his Angel for help, so too in the midst of panic, tragedy, or any nature of need, it is truly right to call upon the Angels. In the darkness of the night, when sleep neglects you, or when you experience the sense of loss, gently close your eyes, slowly breathe in and out a number of times and as you exhale invite the Angels who await your call to surround you. Gently, in a mantra form say: *'Angels come and help me'* or *'God I am ready to embrace my Angel guide'* or a similar short invocation.

> *'So, call upon your Angel when you feel the need*
> *Believe and thank your God above for the Angel*
> *sent in love!'*

However, it is important to note that when first starting to invoke the Angels, it is quite common to encounter a sense of emptiness, of disappointment and disbelief in the perception of the presence of Angels. Do not despair if you do not feel the heavenly presence straight away, you may just need to repeat the exercise until you can feel relaxed enough to let the presence of an Angel to develop, after which the Angelic realm will embody your being. Not everyone will open the energy channel to allow the Angels in!

For some people the concept of Angels does not evolve until some experience gives way to their vulnerability and humility where there individual need is greater than their sense of belief or unbelief. When the Angels attend to our basic needs or step in to save one from a possible accident, tragedy or disaster, we believe in the miraculous work of God through His spiritual aides. It must always be emphasised that when we pray for a miracle and/or ask the Angels to help, we must be patient. We may not always receive the answer we expect; but what we should realise is that the answer to our request will be the right one; it will be what is for one's highest good. For many this concept may prove difficult to accept or understand.

Yet, the outcome in time will become a coherent experience when a better comprehension will be recognised and some sense of reasoning will become apparent allowing the initial anger, disappointment and/ or let down to mean something. Such gives way to the awareness, acceptance and appreciation of the healing power of the Angels. As previously mentioned, knowing when to call the Angels is not that clear cut. Sometimes calling an Angel may occur unconsciously. When Madge was badly hurt in a long and difficult relationship, she didn't realise that the tears, pain and the angst she patiently endured would eventually give way to her calling out to

God in her distress. Madge realised that to heal she needed to surrender her concerns to God.

"Sometimes, I just went along to the Chapel and sat alone in the silence . . . I felt lost. It was as if I was just floating along. I couldn't even pray, I couldn't find words to describe my inner pain . . . I just sat there". Madge exclaimed that out of the silence came a tender voice which filled her with a renewed sense of hope. *"In the silence of the dim lit Chapel, I was aware of a lovely presence . . . a ray of light shone upon the altar . . . I saw a lovely faint image of my mother who had passed away a year ago. Her smile was warm. Reaching out towards me she told me: 'All will be fine, just trust in God'. As I gazed upon her faint image as it began to slip away I cried sorely, my heart was breaking. Then all of a sudden something beautiful happened: no words can describe the peace that I experienced. I felt a happiness I hadn't experienced for years . . . I knew the Angels were with me. The spiritual presence of my mother overwhelmed me and convinced me that good would prevail. There are indeed Angels."*

Just as Madge had described, how many times have we encountered a situation where we experience something extraordinary which is difficult to explain.

The main thing is to be aware, accept and appreciate the presence of the Angels. It is also important to remember that we may call upon the Angels in a conscious or unconscious manner. The Angels are always near. They are ready to respond. In silent brokenness the Angels are sensitive to the call for help. Angels serve to bring that which is for our highest good. So call upon your Angels. God in his goodness wants to support and guide us—His creation.

Do not be afraid!

Call in the dark, in the light, in the silence, in the disquiet or indeed, even in your dreams. When we are open to God's Spirit, healing will occur. When we trust and rely upon God's love; we can believe and experience the gift of real hope.

Healing through the Angels comes about as an answer to one's call.

God always hears our cry, our request and determines what is for our highest good. Sometimes without realising it, we frequently pray for help.

Trust!

Trust and believe.

Trust in the healing power of the Angels.

Healing through the Angels

Healing of self is an extraordinary gift. We are encouraged to surrender to God and hand over that which it is too difficult to do; to accept that there are things we cannot do; and to have the wisdom to know the difference.

If we believe and trust, it is possible to surrender our inabilities to God. However, believing is one of the hardest things to do. When healing occurs, a sense of ease is found. God, through the power of the Angels, heals those who call. Yet, sometimes we are blind to the healing taking place. When the *'dis'* is taken out of 'diseased', we are left with *'eased'* and healing occurs. Sometimes the healing manifests itself in death, where the self is relieved of pain and suffering which cannot be cured.

On a personnel note, it was not easy to accept that I needed help, not just medical help but spiritual help also. After attending doctors and hospitals for many years, my ultimate request for improved health was handed over with complete trust to my Guardian Angel and the help of Archangel Raphael, *'the healer'*.

In a surprisingly short space of time a positive outcome had been granted. Surgery was undertaken and the physical problem was addressed successfully. Such is a result of my renewed and subsequent belief and trust in God and in the healing power of His Angels.

The phenomenon of healing is a difficult concept to explain. Yet without fear of contradiction I have received such powerfully positive answers to my prayers. I have personal experience and awareness of the healing power of the Angels. At the most unexpected moments the presence of the Angels can be overwhelming and there is no doubt that God is near. A few years ago I collapsed in our local Church.

I can remember within my mind calling out for help. *"Nobody seemed to hear me, I fell. Suddenly there were people all around me. Even though I tried to speak, the words just wouldn't come out. I could hear what they were saying but I could not speak. Frustrated and inwardly annoyed, I asked God to help. then, as I lay on the cold ground before the altar, the ambience was extraordinary. It seemed that I was in a tunnel of brilliant white light. I was so peaceful and I didn't want to be moved. I just wanted to stay in that place of serenity. I became aware that a doctor had arrived; he leant down, spoke gently to me, reassuring me that I would be well before he rang for an ambulance. There was a brilliant light around his head and it just seemed that it was God Himself"*. A few weeks later the doctor who attended me on that day was tragically killed and there is no doubt in my mind that he is with God in Heaven. He was the healing Angel who brought me back to life.

'The aura around him will forever be a vision that I will never forget. It is true, that some people leave their imprints upon us!'

As we all know human relationships can prove to be problematic from time to time and indeed one request for help eventually proved positive after what seemed to be a testing period. Morrie told me this anecdote. She started tentatively: *"You know I met what I had perceived to be a lovely couple. It never fails to surprise me how wrong we can be at times. We, well I thought, we became good friends. Through times the relationship grew sour and there was a nasty breakup. Never will I understand why this happened. Frequently, we are so blind to the hidden agendas people bring into relationships.*

It was as if someone had died. I thought I would never get over this but you know what? After a time of prayer and daily communication with the Angels as in the words of 'Julian of Norwich and Teresa of Avilla, all this will pass' this did pass and I found a sense of Peace too wonderful to describe."

After humble surrender of the situation and patiently waiting, the door of peace and communication was fully opened. Through the invocation of Archangel Gabriel, lines of communication allowed a number of issues to be aired and eventually resolved.

Morrie's story is another example of the healing power of the Angels by the action of the Archangels, Michael, Gabriel and Raphael who heard her call, accepted her total surrender and took her concerns to God. An answer to Morrie's prayerful request was undoubtedly received when the deepest sense of peace eradicated what appeared to be an insurmountable state of conflict. A lesson to be learnt was that, as in healing and miracles, all things come to those who wait. *Nothing lasts forever*!

This too shall pass

Miracles and healing are essentially related to the faith and hope within, and therefore, we must never take anything for granted.

Be thankful!

Say 'Thank You'.

I began to relearn the importance of remembering to be thankful to God and appreciative of the spiritual guides which have been sent to assist me on my journey. Throughout life, the Angelic presence comes to us in various forms sometimes in the most unlikely or unexpected ways.

Angelic Presence

After the death of my aged mother, (my closest friend and confidant), my overall well-being became anaemic. While the physical and psychological therapies such as reflexology, acupuncture, herbal medication and counselling nourished my weaknesses, I could not satisfy my spiritual hunger. There was just something missing. Suddenly, while going through my deceased mother's belongings I came across a book on *'Angels'*. I scanned its contents and realised that a gift had come my way. I received an affirmation and a directive. I was trying to make a decision about my desire to write a book about my experiences and stories given to me by like-minded people. This really was a sign that this secret desire to share my interest about the Angels was to be undertaken but not without discernment and prayerful guidance.

At this time a close friend of mine appreciated my interest in wanting to know more and learn about the concept of Angels and God's powerful healing. Together we read and shared many articles written about the power of God's messengers and the Angelic realm. Frequently, I prayed and asked the Angels for affirmation to enable me to believe and trust in the powerful healing of Angels. Quite a number of messages were given to me. Through time a considerable amount of things began to occur. Initially, I was reluctant to speak of such. I wondered if these were just coincidental! *No.* Too many of the insights, visions, whatever they are called were real; there was nothing imaginary about them.

An elderly aunt was dying in hospital, sitting by her bedside holding her hand while my husband sat opposite. I heard what I assumed was the door opening. I indicated such in a silent manner but my husband hadn't notice anything. As I sat still, I felt a hand rest on my shoulder and there was a warm air emanating around me. Then a very tired Aunt N looked up as if she saw someone by me and she lifted her eyes and whispered *"Mary. Mary. I love you"*. Lifting her head and fixing her eyes ahead, it seemed Aunt N was following someone or something moving towards the door which then closed shut. A few hours later Aunt N died and I have no doubt that Our Lady accompanied to her Heavenly home.

The presence of the Angels is not something that just happens. Spiritual renewal and development have a huge part to play. God in His love for us is always ready to listen to our call. I often had the experience of sitting alone in the Chapel or in a quiet space where I experienced the presence of peace, of love and serenity. In this place of stillness and silence I realise I am in God's presence. God wants us to believe that He is there for us in our good times and those not so good times. From a personal perspective, I am in no doubt that I have received many favours granted through Angelic healing. In peaceful serenity and trust I give myself to God.

A few years ago while in Medjugorje on pilgrimage climbing the long trek bare foot up Krizevac (Cross Mountain) a path lined with the Stations of the Cross, Maura told me how she lost her way three times. *"I seemed to veer off to the right. I couldn't see any signs or directions. There was no-one on the path. The silence was overwhelming. The view was astonishing. Suddenly a man whom I can only describe as very European came running up behind me. He was calling in broken English: "Lady, beautiful lady, you are on the wrong path, turn back now" and indicated the way back to the twisting path.*

To say I was shocked would be an understatement. I was taken aback! The man had a strong masculine appearance, quite bald and wearing a short sleeved shirt, stone coloured slacks and sandals, yet, what seemed odd was that he was carrying a brief case and running along a path he which he indicated to be a dead end!

I made my way back onto the main path. A short way further along the path I got lost again. This time I was scared, I really felt trapped and as I looked around I couldn't see any way out.

I was just about to cry when I saw a yellow rose growing out through a rock and I knew I would be alright, St. Therese would look after me.

Eventually, after scrambling through a maze of briars and dry ground covered in thorns I made my way back onto the main path. The first person I met was an old woman who was having difficulty making her way down the path of boulders and loose sand. I couldn't ignore her. I stopped with her. I then gave her my walking stick. The old woman hugged me and began to go down the mountain. I stopped. I gazed out over the village of Medjugorje.

As I turned towards the ninth Station of the Cross, I seemed to drift off the main path again. I thought to myself, 'Jesus falls the third time' and sat down. As I got myself calmed down I made my way back to the path where I could hear people praying aloud. As I moved off I got strength to climb the last part of the ascending journey. As I approached the top of the mountain I sat down and prayed. I was tired. I was hungry. I just buried my face in my hands.

All of a sudden a young woman seemed to appear out of nowhere. She was quite beautiful. She was so gentle. She offered me an apple which I gratefully accepted. We talked, she told me her name was Donna. She said she was from Nova Scotia and I excitedly talked of Fr. Thomas Keating whom I had met in Belfast at a Contemplative Prayer Conference. Just as swiftly as she had appeared, Donna disappeared. I was beginning to think it was all an illusion.

Yet, the apple was real.

I was alone. The peace was awesome.

After a final prayer, I made my way down the twisting path trying to convince myself that I wasn't imagining these happenings; praising God and thanking the Angels who assisted me on my spiritual quest."

A few years later Maura returned to Medjugorje to complete her pilgrimage and on her return down the same mountain, the man whom she believed she saw while on pilgrimage a few years earlier was sitting alone on a large rock. She stopped with him and watched as he drew charcoal pictures of the Sacred Heart and Our Lady. Maura's friends, Christine and Susan, witnessed something strange. They are in no doubt that Maura did experience something, but they didn't know what. *'We could see Maura nodding and speaking but we couldn't see anyone!'*

This experience and more, further strengthened Christine and Susan's somewhat fragile and rather sceptical belief in the concept of Angels. There is no doubt in Maura's mind: *'that the Angel was there to reassure her of her quest and that God heard her call'*. Christine interrupted, *'We, that's me and Susan, were down the mountain before Maura. We waited and wondered what she was at, when she went over and sat down on a rock near the bottom of the path. She was talking and nodding . . . but there was nobody visible. To tell the truth we thought she was losing the plot! After a length of time she got up indicating as if suggesting she was going to join us, and as she did so, she leant forward and seemed to be embracing someone . . . but we still couldn't see anybody!*

As Maura came towards us, we were laughing and saying, 'What were you at?' She calmly replied, 'I was speaking to the man whom I have met before, you know, the man I told you about, the man who put me back onto the path when I got lost the last time I was here'. Then she showed us a beautiful charcoal drawing of Our Lady which this invisible person gave to her. The truth is that we just thought this was weird. A chill ran along my spine as the drawing was real!'

On returning to the house and talking about what had happened, we were convinced that Maura had indeed met an Angel and the drawing was a gift from God.' Maura's story is just one of many that those who are comfortable with: the awareness, acceptance and appreciation of the Angels, their function and their empowerment are willing to share. Christine's, on the other hand, is an example of an experience which strengthened her resolve to explore the concept of the Angels.

Such examples reinforce the profound belief that Angels come to us.

Angels do come—just call!

Angels come to us . . .

When we are blessed with good health, wealth and happiness the presence of such Angelic form may never be recognised. For many this may seldom feature with any relevance at all in their lives; but Angels do exist and they are there ready to act. God's Heavenly Messengers, Angels, Guides, Protectors are spiritual ministers assigned to us.

At least one Angel will guard and protect each soul from the moment of one's conception to the moment of one's departure from this earthly habitat and it is possible that another Angel is assigned to be the quiet one who stands by. Therefore, each of us has at least two Angels: one Angel who serves as a result of being ever vigilant, with an active energy of guidance and protection; the other Angel with an energy that is quietly poignant and unassuming. This guardian waits patiently on your invocation or invitation for help. Angels come to us if we dare to trust. Angels come to us in various ways.

Angels may come to us in the form of a fellow human being, as an animal or as an energy or presence. In essence, within the realm of spiritual growth it is the responsibility of each of us to appreciate and embrace the great gift of loving care and protection, given to us from God, in the form of the Angels who wish to assist in bringing about the highest good for each of us. In bringing about the love and highest good for each person one at a time, the world continues to evolve as a better and more harmonious planet.

Therefore, we are fortunate and blessed to be the recipients of the powerful healing of the Angels, a heavenly energy that empowers and embodies our quest for complete well-being. For many people, Angels are called upon through childhood years as parents and siblings together in morning and night prayers ask for the guidance and protection of God's heavenly realm. The welcoming image of a beautiful Angel is for many an image that is easy to recollect. A simple elegant image of a feathered winged figure symbolises the presence of an Angel. Despite that fact many authors argue that Angels do not have wings, for many this is a common image.

Yet, the image of fan-shaped feather coated wings, offers a sense of being caressed, embraced by God, providing a sense of serenity and security.

'Oh! Angels of God's Heavenly realm spread
your wings of love around;'

Ultimately, the belief and acceptance of one's Angel is an individualistic choice. For most of us, the tender years of adolescence, followed by adult years, was directed by a means of various demands which silently take control of our lives and the simple practice of calling on God's Angels are unintentionally forgotten.

Yet

'God is watching over me, through you, my Angel'. The Angels are waiting!

Within the span of life, short term or long, each individual life takes control of the driving wheel of life at some stage and sometimes God takes a back seat. When we are well, healthy, and wealthy and secure, we may unintentionally forget that life cannot be fulfilled without the presence of God. It's hard to realise that inner well-being is an essential requisite for living and through time the lack of nourishment and support of the soul yields to a weakening and depletion of ultimate wellbeing, when body, soul and/or mind begin to deteriorate.

Therefore, it seems fair to suggest that every individual has a story full of mystery to share. Yet, how frequently do we ever take the opportunity to notice the velocity and extent of life experiences being lived out day by day, week by week, month by month, and reeling swiftly into unseen years lost as a consequence of life's demands.

The mundane day-to-day duties and the ordinary demands which we encounter each day, the drama of life and living which Karl Rahner referred to as *'the theatre of God's grace'*. Through each day we pray for the grace of God, and in acts in which we seek help and assistance. In recognising our need for help we can become aware of the healing power of the Angels.

Do we dare to help ourselves?

Do we dare to believe and embrace the concept of the healing power of the Angels?

Healing power of the Angels!

The concept of healing in contemporary society has become more widely regarded as being legitimate and possible. The healing power of the Angels is becoming more acceptable. The fear of what other people think is not as powerful as it had been for generations. The empowerment of self belief is a contemporary reflection of the awareness, acceptance and acknowledgement that we are entitled to all that is good. God's healing power brings about balance and wholeness and healing which interplay between divine compassion and human need.

In today's world for many people, there is a desire to seek instant answers, extraordinary and sometimes unrealistic and somewhat dramatic healings from medical and spiritual interventions. People want everything to be fixed instantly. Indeed there may very well be stories of instant healing as for some healing may involve immediate relief as a result of the high intensity of profound belief. Yet, for most there is a need for patience.

Thus healing, the healing power of the Angels, has become worthy of respectful attention and acceptance to be a more credible remedy in relation to spiritual nourishment and the culmination of ultimate well-being. Angels may never be seen but their presence is very surreal.

The gift God gives is a fundamental, yet, unseen aide, to the human creation which assists and guides us as we confront the challenging journey upon earth. This concept is almost too marvellous to imagine. The vague and unseen presence of the Angelic aide is a powerful energy, quietly and patiently waiting to guide and assist when called upon. The healing power of the Angels is more powerful than one can ever begin to imagine. God empowers each and every one of us. These unseen and unheard guides readily respond to any call for help. Angels do come to us, just call upon the Angels and you too will experience the loving healing energy of God.

We have the choice.

We all have 'free will'.

God's love is unconditional, He will respond.

Healing may be the return to physical health; a renewed sense of self; mental stability, or being given the peace to accept that the greatest gift may be the release to eternal life. The essential realisation is that no prayer goes unanswered. We always will receive that which is for one's highest good. Healing is brought about as a result of various factors as simple as a placebo effect, and/or with profound faith and sheer self determination to obtain the best for self.

The process of healing requires constancy of care, confidence and belief, especially relevant when vulnerable, anxious or insecure!

When a physical and/or psychological cure cannot be realised a spiritual healing is still possible and its worth cannot be underestimated: the power is congruent, balanced and based ultimately on God's love, love which is the energy that connects the body, mind and soul.

Healing is rarely instantaneous.

Healing is gradual in nature.

The healing process is not one of creating a readymade cure. It is not straightforward; it doesn't just happen. Healing may be achieved when we are prepared and ready to receive. Indeed, many people may never receive or experience the cure they seek. In some instances people have expressed their experience as finding an unexpected sense of serenity that enables them to accept God's will.

Anna who had a terminal condition found a great sense of hope despite her diagnosis: *"When I was told that I had a short time to live, I was devastated. I cried for days. Then one day at the hospital for a routine treatment, I met another woman who was in a similar situation. She was so pleasant. Light shone out of her being. Her eyes were bright and alive even though her body was frail and pale. We talked about life, family and then about hobbies! Hobbies, I looked at her as if she weren't wise. I am dying, that's all I could think of! I really wondered how she could be so upbeat. As her name was called by the nurse, we said goodbye. While I waited for my call, I began to think of what we were talking about. A little voice inside my head provoked me to consider the positive attitude of that woman. This wonderful experience allowed me to respond creatively and peacefully to a chronic or terminal health condition. Angels came to me in all sorts of ways; on gift cards, prayer cards, figurines, candles and within people I met".* Such a realisation and recognition that Angels exist requires openness, patience, trust and acceptance towards something of that which is not tangible or observable.

So often, we believe that if we cannot see something specific then it cannot exist. This belief reflects the doubt which St. Thomas experienced: this disciple of Jesus did not believe that Christ had risen from the dead. Such was an example of human weakness which was healed when

Jesus appeared in the upper room. There Jesus invited Thomas to touch the wounds of his hands, his feet and his side and said, *'Happy are those who have not seen and yet believe'*.

Therefore, in a sense, it is fair to suggest that we too are being invited to trust that God heals and akin to St. Thomas, when we doubt we are invited to savour the healing essence which enables us to attain peaceful wholeness.

As stated before, each of us has at least one Angel. For many it is accepted that we have two Angels ultimately assigned to care and protect us on our journey upon this planet. One at each shoulder, one to the right and one to the left! Angels come in various form, symbols, presence, energy and harmony as exemplified by Anna's testimony.

I have been blessed to have had many encounters with my Angels. I have two Angels with me all times. While it is generally agreed that there is no gender appropriated to Angels, in my case, I have a male and a female Angel. I have an Angel at my right shoulder and a female at my left. Archangel Michael is robust and giant-like in stature; he spreads his awesome span of protection around me. Archangel Ariel in her femininity rests her motherly presence and protection around me. And a third Angel has more recently become apparently responsive to me. Archangel Metatron's white light of protection is always present. Frequently, powerful colours of yellow and red comfort and secure me. Intermittently, spheres of green and blue lights merge reflecting the healing power of God. The energy seeps into me and revitalises my inner self.

While in Medjugorje, a Grey Friar, whom I had never encountered before, prayed with me; after a period of meditation he told me that I have two spiritual guides,

Ascended Masters; St. Therese also known as 'the Little Flower' and Mother Teresa of Calcutta. I was so excited: this was an affirmation. I have always held a special place in my heart for St. Therese and greatly admire the humble and compassionate nature of Mother Teresa of Calcutta. Whow! Even in this I believed that the Angels were working.

Quite often, Angels are neither seen nor heard but their presence is always felt. Permitting the Angels to become actively involved in life and living brings a depth of integrated energy. This awakens and releases the past drawing on the present, allowing the cellular memory to let go, to release and to absorb a new way of life.

In the great belief of the Angels we can experience how they work effortlessly to please, to help and support all of God's creation. Angels may appear in visions, images surreal and gentle or in noises soft and sweet, melodious and upbeat.

Mary asked if she could share her story regarding her narrow escape at the Mall. *"I was walking through the Mall. I thought I heard my name being called. When I turned around there was no-one there. Again I thought I heard my name being called but still it seemed there was no-one there. When I turned back out of the side of my eye I saw the reflection of a young man coming up behind me. As he approached he tried to snatch my handbag. I reacted so quickly he didn't have a chance. I was amazed at my swift reaction. Afterwards I convinced myself that the voice I had heard was the voice of my Angel. It was a warning which helped me to be vigilant and alert. If I hadn't seen the young man's reflection in the shop window I possibly would not have stopped him".*

So take comfort. When that which is unseen or unheard is present, there is an Angel therein!

Angels Unseen, Unheard

How do we dare to believe in that which we cannot see? How do we understand visions which occur? How do we recognise that which is real and that which is an illusion?

Images may be real.

Angels may be seen.

Angels may not be seen but felt.

A feather can be enough to be aware of an Angel.

Angels create a warm soft ambience.

Angels work to please.

Angels are non-judgemental.

Angels are ready to help.

Angels work unconditionally to enhance and beautify the world.

Angels offer so much to life and living!

How do we distinguish between what we hear, what we think we hear and what is unheard?

What we hear or think we hear is characterised and inspired by God: when we experience a good sense of consistency, motivation, tone, origin and familiarity, believe.

Confidence, acceptance and acknowledgement of Divine guidance may be apparent through dreams, feelings, visions, symbols, signs, and vibrant cheerful lights and colours.

While we try to interpret that which we hear the Angels can help to direct our enquiring and questioning spiritual hunger. These Angels wait attentively for our call. They, the messengers of God, readily respond when called upon!

They are beings that reside by us.

While they are unseen and unheard, their presence is undeniably felt. The presence of someone near; the unseen, unheard spirits accompany us. There is something awesome about the silence and that which is heard in that place.

Indeed, we may call upon as many Angels as we want to assist us. We can ask for one, two, three . . . hundreds and more, all of which have the healing power of God to help heal personal issues of the past; heal and embrace the present and with our approval may aim to assist us with an easier transition into the future segments of life and living. As God has granted each of us the gift of *'freewill'*, it is important to note that the Angels can't intervene or help without an invitation to do so, except in extreme life threatening situations in which our Angels have a duty to guide and protect us from danger.

Angels desire to bring about happiness and peace into our world creating a peaceful place for all. Love, peace and sincere belief enable harmony to be realised where hope can enhance life and living!

It is generally accepted that Angels are more often *'unseen, unheard'*. Yet, Angels are everywhere; they, the Angels, are actively working to bring about ultimate peace and happiness to the Earth and to all who inhabit the Earth. According to one of the great spiritual leaders, St. Thomas Aquinas *'all the extraordinary gifts of grace in the Church are appropriated to the Holy Spirit who communicates them through the Angels'.* The whole life of the Church and humanity benefits from the mysterious and powerful help of the Angels. Again, St. Thomas Aquinas points to the need of the divine help of the Angels: *'Man cannot progress to merit except by divine help, which is extended to man by means of the ministry of the Angels'.*

However, for most the notion that, that which is Divine, that which is invisible seems a ludicrous ordeal, a somewhat crazy undertaking. With faith, with trust, with hope anything can be achieved. When God is at the centre everything else falls into place; true it may take time, but, what is time? Time is an instant, a phase, a period which like all things will pass. With patience the result will yield fruit in plenty. Angels wait. God waits. We too are challenged to wait. Good things come to those who wait.

The unseen, unheard ministers of the spirit heal our brokenness and our pain when we surrender our concerns to God. The Archangels joyfully bring God's grace and blessing to we who call.

Unseen, Unheard!

Through the ambience of tranquil peace
God's presence enraptures, me, you!
Angels wait in awesome patient mood
to hear the call from me, you!
Waiting quietly, prepared to act
God's messengers are there for me, you!
Unseen, unheard, this Special one
awaits to respond to me, you!

As Angels directed from God above
watch and listen to me, you!
Such Special beings cannot act alone
but in response to me, you!
God's gift of gentle tenderness
is there for me, you!
And so one must be prepared
to accept God's gift for me, you!

Angels waiting in silent watch
guard constantly over me, you!
Angelic presence, God's gift of love
is there for me, you!
As a feather fluttering in the breeze
the sign is there for me, you!
Waiting quietly, prepared to act
God's messengers are there for me, you!

*Unseen, unheard, this Special one awaits
to respond to me, you!*

When you call upon the Angels for help, their response is immediate despite the fact that we sometimes don't have the trust and patience required to notice this. As answers to our requests may frequently come to us in an unexpected way, sometimes it takes time to realise and accept that this has in actual fact been granted.

All requests to God are answered. No prayer goes unanswered; but frequently the answers do not come about just the way we want. Yet the answer will always prove to be right for you, even if it takes time for one to appreciate and accept it to be so! When we surrender that which we cannot do ourselves, that which we cannot change or amend, the favourable outcome will be realised sooner. When we trust, and surrender our concerns to the Angels who take all to God on our behalf, the reward will surely be great. Our personal thoughts, prayers, meditations and desires contribute to the field energies that enable a person's ability to find an almost perfect peaceful wholeness. Thus, one may experience a profound emotional, physical and spiritual transformation.

This reminds me of the *'Prayer of Serenity'* in which we are invited to have the wisdom to hand all that which we cannot do, that which we cannot change over to God: *'Lord, grant me the grace to Accept the things I cannot change, Courage to change the things I can and Wisdom to know the difference.'*

Restoration

Healing in its most basic sense is restoration. To heal is to restore. Healing irrespective of body, mind and/or soul cannot happen without interrelated sources of support. Healing of the physical self may be achieved by a means of using traditional, complementary and/or alternative medicine or a combination of various medicinal methods. While the spiritual aspect of life requires the regular use of personal prayer, it also benefits from the active and compassionate prayerful support of family, friends and community.

From early childhood years we are encouraged to kneel down by the bedside in the morning to pray for help and support to bring us through the day; at night we were encouraged to kneel by the bedside and say a prayer of thanksgiving for the day coming to an end. The challenge continues to invite us to practise morning and evening prayer. The perseverance to believe and practise the simple act to pray is a valuable contribution to the sustenance needed to sustain the health of the soul. So healing of the soul may come about with a very simple approach where the Angels can assist our quest.

So how can healing of the soul come about?

Is spiritual healing possible?

What are the tools available to bringing about a balance of spiritual well-being?

The request for the healing power of Angels through quiet or vivacious invocation is an essential element to spiritual development.

Yet, it is also true, that depending on the time and need for assistance, Angelic invocations may not always be made with quiet gentleness but with a sense of anger, fear and/or disbelief. The bridge between belief and disbelief in the power of the Angels is quite fragile. On one side it may not be macho to surrender to the simplicity and patient acceptance of something that is unseen or unheard; yet, this may be a powerful energy beneficial to wholeness of self. While on the other side of the bridge it may be easy to perceive that there is an inexplicable yet miraculous presence; energy powerfully experienced within the everyday existence of life and living.

A new acceptance of spirituality has come about with the notion that Angels, who are messengers of God, can bring about powerful healing which enhances our chance to experience an almost perfect and ultimate well-being. As people have become more independent in their thinking, a greater openness and perception of spiritual development has encouraged and challenged many to search and explore various avenues, in which they nourish, maintain and sustain complete well-being.

In contemporary society, people want to choose, select and make up their own minds as to what therapies they feel are of value and which can enhance their individual needs, suitable to their personal life style and living. Therefore, in order to understand the healing power of the Angels, it is important to explore the concept of spirituality, the existence of Angels and the functions of such spiritual beings in relation to achieving ultimate well-being. Each of us at some point in our personal lives or possibly at many intersections of life, seek answers to the small, yet, powerful questioning word, 'why'?

Frequently we ask Why? Why me? Why us?

We consistently seek and find, sometimes with great trepidation, sometimes with great ease; for each and everyone the answers to our quests do occur, but for some the answers may not come the way we anticipate or not within the time scale we envisage. Indeed the outcome may be swift or may be quite the opposite and take quite a long time but what is for sure is that the answer will inevitably become apparent in time. In our basic humanity, we often feel we need to drive the response rate, we want to do the driving, dictate the answer and outcome expecting the answer to be the way we want it to be and within the time scale we dictate. The ego continues to be in conflict. 'Easing God out' the ego tries to drive the vehicle of life and living without the direction of God.

Search for wholeness

In today's society everything is readily available; we live in world dictated by the concept of supply and demand. Often confused the challenge is to be open to the notion that the economy cannot supply the demands of the needs necessary for ultimate well-being. Very often, many of us experience a point in life where a sense of burn-out may occur: a familiar component of life as a consequence of the complexity of modern day living. In the human make up there are various segments to be nourished: body, soul and mind.

Physical image may be enhanced with the products provided by the economic services. One of the greatest therapies which have developed in contemporary society is associated with physical image. While body image is important, there is the need to accept that the care of the body must include the mind and the soul. Beauty and all that such encompasses can only be achieved when all parts of the human self are catered for! When all parts are working in harmony, the beauty of every human being is clearly seen which presents a person of wholeness, happiness and peace. This may be evident when light and joy shine through those we meet.

For ultimate well-being, there has been a great emphasis put onto the search for the physical and psychological therapies which have developed in recent times; therapies in which various practitioners offer treatment to enhance the wellbeing of the body and the mind, using treatments and tools for individuals to experience and to personally use to enhance one's well being. Generally it's accepted that such mechanisms and therapeutic instruments offer help to nourish and support one's overall wellbeing, but without all parts being cared for, ultimate well-being cannot be achieved.

Therefore, it is important to ask what about the well-being of one's spiritual self, the soul?

Angelic Realm

The Angelic realm is a composite of a range of Angels. There are numerous guides, too many to mention in this short piece of work. The main substance of healing is to be found within the realm of the Archangels, four of which are most familiar to many of us: Archangels Gabriel, Michael, Raphael and Uriel. Until very recently there were only three Archangels frequently mentioned: the three Archangels called upon most often are—Michael, Raphael and Gabriel. In more recent times the recognition of Archangel Uriel has become more apparent. Each of these Archangels has specific roles in relation to guidance and protection but their responsibilities are solely to serve and to bring about that which is for one's highest good.

These Archangels when called upon, even if working with another human being can assist with one's quest. Archangels have the ability to simultaneously hear and answer without disturbing or detracting from the needs of the other person. Archangel Gabriel, is the bringer of healing focusing within the sphere of communication: Archangel Michael who is the defender, is the Angel who is one of protection and peace, God's aide who helps to elevate fear: Archangel Raphael, who brings God's healing, while Archangel Uriel brings light from afar unto difficult situations. Angels are the lowest rank within the Angel hierarchy. Angels are assigned to human beings even before birth, from the moment of conception.

Angels may even take on a human appearance and connect with us as we journey throughout life and living as revealed in the Sacred Scriptures, Book of Tobit, where the Archangel Raphael took on a human form while protecting Tobias the son of Tobit.

Many Angels are unemployed and are happy to be called upon. Can you imagine that? All we have to do is call *'Angel'* and God's help is at hand. There are people whom we encounter who just seem to have that which we would love to have, that sense of peacefulness and serenity, that easy ability to express their profound belief and trust that everything will work out. It would seem fair to suggest that such qualities are of a spiritual nature, qualities personified within and as a consequence of the deity of heaven.

Therefore, while it is generally accepted that Angels are heavenly beings which we may rarely recognise, it is true that we may very well encounter Angels, human beings who work to make life better for others, who give without quest, who give and do not count the cost, those who quietly help and support without looking for notice or reward. So in everyday encounters you may well be entertaining Angels as reflected in the story of Dorothy Day! Whether visible or audible, it is a great spiritual support to know that *Angels do exist!* The invitation to call upon Angels is for everyone, irrespective of creed or culture. Everyone has the gift of choice. It is an individual prerogative as to whether we believe in Angels or not! Sometimes in the best or not so good experiences of life it is a valuable support to be open to the invocation of the spiritual assistance of God. Within every experience, whether good or bad, there is a reason. Nothing just happens. Even if we are not aware, the Angels know what is to become of every experience. It is we who have the choice to ignore or to believe that something good will eventually emerge in time.

Mary offered her anecdote: *"I was badly hurt. I was falsely accused of that which I had not done! I felt abused and used. I just could not understand why this should be . . . I was angry, annoyed and badly hurt. I called to God in my despair.*

Why me?

I just could not believe that the very people I had helped and supported could turn so viscously and attack me. For months I could not sleep. I could not eat. I was at a loss; the negative effect was gnawing away at my inner peace. The experience was impacting upon my inner strength. My heart and soul hurt so much; it was as if my heart and soul were destroyed. Eventually, life within me began to grow again, my heart no longer ached; my soul began to live again. I wasn't nervous anymore. Even though I knew I was innocent, the terror almost killed me. What kept me going was the belief that God would see me through this awful ordeal. I had no doubt that the Angels were with me. What seemed so bad actually gave way to a greater sense of belief. Life and living are difficult enough, so I decided not to fight back. I just prayed for those who persecuted me. I found great peace and thank the Angels everyday. I have loads of feathers which I found when I was going through this painful period of conflict; ironically, simple feathers were of powerful support to me. In the midst of all the fear and anxiety the presence of a lone feather provided so much affirmation. Yeah, I know, for some this may seem strange, but when in need the littlest of things can actually be so meaningful and supportive.

Angels, yes, Angels do exist".

Mary's story was a reflection of an encounter in which a negative experience gave way to a positive outcome. Mary became a stronger person because of the journey she had endured due to the concealed abhorrence of others. In the time of her painful experience, Mary said that she had depended solely on God. Every day, she called upon the Angels. *'Without the Angels I never would have survived'*, Mary said with a gentle quiver in her voice . . . . she continued *'Archangels were busy responding to my constant needs. Michael strengthened me, I was aware of his protection, Raphael embodied my weak physical state with a healing energy so wonderful. Gabriel through words of comfort and spiritual communication empowered me to further trust in a good conclusion. With a thousand Angels of various dominions, the Angels surrounded me, supported me and sheltered me.*

You have no idea how much I depended on the Angels . . . God has given me so much. I could never have gotten through all this without the wonderful messengers God sent to me.'

Choirs of Angels

There are nine choirs of Angels. Within this compilation there are three hierarchies—

1st hierarchy-Seraphim, Cherubim and Thrones

2nd hierarchy-Dominions, Virtues, Powers

3rd hierarchy-Principalities, Archangels and Angels

GOD is central within the Choirs of Angels.

The *'Seraphim'* are the highest order of Angels who are guardians or attendants about the throne of God. As sited in Isaiah 6:1-7, the Seraphim praise God calling *'Holy, Holy, Holy, Lord God of Hosts'*. The *'Cherubim'* symbolise God's power and glory and are second highest of the nine choirs of Angels. Within the New Testament the Cherubim are alluded to as celestial attendants within the Book of the Apocalypse. *'Thrones'* are next in order and reflect humility, submission and Peace. Angels of the lower ranks need Thrones in order to access God.

Within the second hierarchy of Choirs, *'Dominions'* oversee the duties of the Angels and are referred to as the Angels of Leadership. *'Virtues'* govern nature and are known as the *'Spirits of Motion'*; they have control over the seasons, stars, the moon and the sun. These Angels are sometimes referred to as the *'shinning ones'*. Virtues provide grace, courage and valour and are in charge of miracles. The choir of *'Powers'* are Warrior Angels that fight to defend of the cosmos and humanity; they are protectors against evil who attempt to create chaos and destruction through human beings.

Within the third hierarchy of Angels, *'Principalities'* are referred to within the New Testament as one type of spiritual being, in other words they are metaphysical. *'Archangels'* are generally referred to as *'chief'* Angels. They have a unique role as God's messengers to people when in need. While it is agreed that there are seven Archangels, not all lists include the same names. However, there are four which always appear in all lists of Archangels: Michael, Raphael, Gabriel and Uriel. Finally, *'Angels'* are listed as the lowest rank, yet, are the spiritual beings which people most frequently call upon. These Angels are closest to the world and therefore are closest to human beings. They serve with love. They deliver the requests of human beings to God and are the bringers of news and answers in return.

Within the Catholic Church there is a prayer dedicated to St. Michael the Archangel, the defender against evil and there is also a Chaplet of St. Michael both of which are printed at the end of this book. We all need protection; these prayers are not solely for the use of Catholics but are available to all who seek to use them. No prayer is ever wasted, no prayer is ever unanswered.

Archangels

Archangels are powerful protectors and overseers of other Angels. They manage and direct Angels to protect and heal human beings. They lead Angels who desire to please God in serving human beings, God's creation. It is generally agreed between various groups and faith traditions that there are four, maybe seven Archangels, we have become familiar with four: Archangels Michael, Raphael, Gabriel and Uriel. Each one has a particular role and carry out specialised functions.

Michael means *'he who is of God'* or *'one who looks like God'* whose aim is to dispose of fear and plant joy. Michael is the leader of God's army. He is the supreme commander of the Heavenly Hosts. Energy colour associated with Michael the Archangel is blue; dark peacock, turquoise and shimmering tones of bright stark neon light.

Archangel Raphael refers to the healing force of God. Raphael means *'God heals'*. The energy colours associated with Raphael are various shades of green; predominantly emerald green and hints of pink hues. Archangel Gabriel reflects God's strength.

Gabriel means *'God is my strength'*. Energy colours reflecting the presence of Gabriel are Gold and/or white, bold and bright reflecting confidence and strength.

Archangel Uriel leads us to our destiny. Uriel means *'God is my light'*. And it is not surprising that the energy colours associated with Uriel are shades of purple, pink and magenta.

Within the Roman Catholic Church, the Feast of the Archangels—Michael, Raphael and Gabriel is celebrated on September 29 each year. These three Archangels feature within the Scriptures and are therefore considered within the *'canaconical writings of the Bible'*.

Invitation

As I have discovered through prayer and research, the Angelic Messengers of God are a vital constituent within the healing of soul. I believe that the phenomenon in relation to the concept of Angels to be an enhancement to my desire to experience holistic well-being. *Angels do come—just call!* is an invitation to savour some of that which I have sought, a spiritual healing and support brought about through prayer and humble surrender to unlearn the conditional practices of the past and the openness to embrace a new awareness, acceptance and appreciation of that which serves spiritual wellbeing.

As a consequence of my experience of God's healing through the Angels, I start each day with an invocation, a prayer, calling on my Angel to actively guide and protect me, my family and my friends. Sometimes, I freely believe I can call upon a band of Angels to assist in helping me to face the day awaiting me. I vary the daily practice by silently praying, or simply choosing a piece of scripture on which I meditate, or quietly contemplate the day ahead in which I ask the Angels to rest with me in silence.

The spiritual support helps me to be positive as I face the day ahead. The practice allows me to believe that the Heavenly Angelic realm will protect me. Since embracing the healing power of the Angels, I find myself free of negative people and situations. At the end of day I endeavour to quietly contemplate and thank God for the assistance given to me through the powerful healing of the Angels. While, I would encourage you to consider such a spiritual practice, it would be worth remembering to be patient while acquiring the learning process of the practice. As a means to experiencing spiritual healing it is important to remember that the ultimate goal is to receive that which is for one's highest good, which is what God wishes to give to all.

While on a flight to Rome, a young man situated across from me looked very unsettled. He was very anxious and looked really nervous. I went over to him and asked if I could sit with him for a moment. He admitted that he was terrified of flying. As we talked he seemed to relax. I showed him a book I had with me about spirituality and the power of Angels. He asked if he could borrow the book. As he began to flick through the book, I thought I would go back to my seat and get the book from him when we landed at Rome. Amazingly, his whole appearance changed and he looked at ease. On landing at Rome, he returned the book to me and as we walked to collect our luggage, he shared his view on the subject of spirituality and Angelology: *"I was interested in reading about Angels but I was too macho. Now I would say I was just too much of a coward to be seen reading such. Hey! Thank you so much, I found the book to be something I would now read".* As he handed the book back to me he said, *"Goodbye and thank you again, you have just opened up a new world to me".*

Once again I realised that we can so easily help each other with a simple gesture or a word of affirmation. We are challenged to live what God invites us to do.

Invocation

Begin each day with a prayer, an invocation and a short time of meditation or reflection. God's Heavenly Angels are ready and waiting to guide you through the day, remembering that they can't act or interfere without your call for assistance. It is important that you thank the Angels for their unseen and unheard support, their readiness to help and assistance you receive when the need arises! Like all things in life, it is the routine practice which helps us to realise the gift we receive from God. Meditation and reflection enhance the empowerment to nourish ones' soul.

Physical, psychological and spiritual dimensions of completeness can be achieved through recognition and acceptance of external help. Contemporary therapies offer much in the line of 'New-age' techniques with regard to the concept of ultimate well-being; in which quite often the spiritual element is not recognised as a phenomenon worthy of attention or less worthy of attention. However, I would suggest that the latter is greatly in need of recognition, reaction and due response, as the concept of holistic well-being is a modern day requisite for many.

The words of the Angels

In recognition of the many requests which have been granted and the guidance of my compassionate, understanding and supportive band of Angels, I believe it is appropriate to share the spiritual words of Angelic faith in verse and prose with all who desire to learn of the healing power of God's Heavenly Angels. All words that have come to me in relation to the concept of Angels, the power of Angels, the healing power of the Angels are of awareness, acceptance and appreciation. God alone directs the words of wisdom, the words of faith, hope and love and the words of Angelic service which have been my support and help over the recent years of my life.

It is true that Angels are quick to respond, Angels hear every request and Angels take all that one hands over directly to God. The Heavenly messengers of God are with each and every one of us twenty-four-seven.

While we sleep the Angels guard us from all harm, and while we are awake the Angels silently walk by our sides responding immediately to each call for support and help. In appreciation of the Angels who accompany me and who have accompanied me throughout my younger life, I have respectfully invited you to read and reflect on inspirational and prayerful messages of faith, hope, and love.

So often when I go to start typing it is as if the most beautiful spiritual thoughts flow from my fingertips onto the keyboard. Without doubt I know that such words are words of the Spirit, they are of God. Angels surround my being and guide my writing and compilation of verse.

Oh! Angels sent by God, guide me, support me and direct me, this I pray.

May all you who wish to invoke your Heavenly aides do so without hesitation. Spiritual nourishment is an essential requisite to healthy living. When body, mind and soul are cared for life becomes more grounded and complete. Through the past years I have become more attuned to what God wants me to know, what the Angels want me to hear, that which enhances and benefits my well-being of body, mind and soul.

Enlightenment

The gift of Angelic healing has become a profound part of my life in recent times. Not so long ago, I too, was one of those sceptics who so wanted to believe in the Angels healing power but had difficulty in being open to handing my concerns over without trying to control the response. Yet, I became aware that something powerful was at work when I began to trust in the existence of the Angels, starting with the first test in which I called upon the Angels to show me that they were near. In swift response, either a quiet sense of someone nearby or a feather upon my path reaffirmed me.

Over the past few years ill health took its toll on my physical, psychological and spiritual wellbeing. While many therapies, including reflexology, acupuncture and counselling, were accessible to the enhancement of my physical and psychological wellbeing there was something amiss. Initially I wasn't able to pinpoint what it was; but as a consequence of becoming reawakened to the notion that God speaks to us,

I found great solace and peace. And often recalled the words of Samuel: *"Speak, oh Lord, your servant is listening"*, Mark 2:20-22.

After a time of reflection and acceptance I began to realise that I hadn't really appreciated the need to nourish the spiritual dimension of my life. For some unknown reason I had never had had the need to stop to consider this as an important need in relation to ultimate well-being. I had merely considered that the spiritual side of life was looked after. I always practised my faith. I tried to do what I considered to be required of a good Christian, a good Catholic. I had taken so much for granted.

How then could I address the concept of spiritual wellbeing? After all, I have always carried out my duties of faith to the best of my abilities and so on! Even though I have been blessed to have the gift of a strong loving family circle, the voluntary work carried out alongside daily demands caused me to experience a very profound sense of 'burn-out'. Frequently, I found myself slip into various depths of searching, experiencing feelings of loneliness, fear, worthlessness and emptiness. Within the depth of God's love I welcomed the Angels into my life and living.

Learning to ask

But how do we learn to ask and receive with dignity and respectful patience? If we ask Angels to assist us, then surely we need to submit our quests with trust, allowing them to take our cares to God who in turn will respond with that which is for our highest good. As mentioned before, many of us experience the need for instant response and realise that quite frequently the answer will not be as swift as we want, or the way we want; sometimes we miss the response in that we may be too busy asking and living out commentaries rather than listening, too busy directing and organising rather than waiting or too busy being consumed with self-control and desires that the answer may well be misplaced/overlooked.

Angels who are God's gift to us, offer each and every one of us support, help and comfort, as they lovingly carry our worries, quests and concerns to God. Yet for many this is a difficult concept to accept, to understand and to believe. However, if we think on the parable of the vine, and believe we are but the branches of God's plan, and if we believe that we are an integral part of the vine, how can we doubt that God will not respond in giving the best to us the branches of this spiritual vine? Spiritual formation comes about when we connect with God through the spiritual disciplines in which we experience the energy of the vine: *"I am the vine, you are the branches"*, an energy that enables us to bear much fruit in other words when we connect to the vine, we not only connect with the spirit of Christ but also fellow 'vine-mates'.

Fear

Fear, originates from a negative source. Fear refers to lack of confidence and lack of self-belief which can affect how we react to the challenge to be assertive and brave enough to move outside the norm in order to seek help. For many, personal inner fear of how others react is very influential in relation to personal growth. Experiences of negative events and/or happenings can erode the essence of one's being. For many some past events or experiences may lie somewhere in the back of our minds and can negatively impact on development of well-being. When clouds block out the sun, the light grows dim, so too, when fear is allowed to grow the light within fades. Fear can give way to the emergence of depression, anxiety, panic attacks and more, but, this too can be defeated with the help of the Angels.

If such is not attended to, fear may create a block that will disengage us from reality. Life is reality, reality is life. We have a responsibility to seek that which makes us feel good, look good and act good. The destructive block of hopelessness may cause us to be blind and deaf to what God wants to share with us. This creator, our God, freely offers vital spiritual support and healing through the Angelic realm in which Archangels and Angels are readily available to help to heal our physical, emotional, relationship needs and so much more. Mistrust, fear and disbelief, block our intimate connections with the God and the Angels, which in turn impedes our gift to hearing and receiving the Angel messages, been given to us. When we unblock these negative energies we open ourselves to recognising, appreciating and accepting the gift of spiritual well-being.

The art of Patience

Within our modern world there is a great need for patience. We frequently find it difficult to appreciate that all good things come about in time. When we desire quick answers we are more likely to try to orchestrate the outcome. We become so impatient that the response may become obscure, tainted by our own desired outcome rather than patiently waiting on what God perceives as the best solution or answer to our quest. Even the Angels, yes, the messengers of God, have to practise the art of Patience? It is patience and quiet surrender which enables us to receive and accept the most suitable answer to our prayer, our quest.

As Angels cannot act without our permission (except in extreme danger) they too have to wait quietly upon our call for help. Angels too have to be patient. Therefore, the belief, trust and awareness to the acknowledgement that Angels do exist and that Angels wait upon our call are a concept worthy of consideration. Subsequent trust in acknowledging the great gift of love God wants to share with each and every one of us, Angels who wait:

'Waiting quietly, prepared to act,
God's messengers are there for me, for you!'

Waiting requires patience, a practice which for most is a difficult exercise to realize. For many people the personal inadequacies of not being able to *'fix it'* or *'sort it'* can be very frustrating, as in contemporary society many people own the need to be in control which in itself creates a false sense of self. Yet, with patience and careful acceptance of the need for help and the understanding that we do not have the ability to do everything or fix everything will develop in time, even though there will still be people who will we still expect everything with a sense of immediacy. We have to learn to surrender and wait with faith without trying to direct how and when answers to our quests come about.

To learn demands us to unlearn, and you rightly ask: *'How do we unlearn?'* Sometimes we learn through life's experience and this is not necessarily correct depending on the situation and/or the needs in relation to particular needs or situations. How many times have any of us believed and said *'sure I know how to do that'* or *'sure I could fix that'*? The thing is we all need to remember that we are not God. Therefore, take time to unlearn and relearn how to be aware, accept and appreciate a new approach to embracing that which we cannot see!

Life and living is essentially quite a complex and sensitive feature that requires a person to unlearn the lack of care given to oneself. For many the need to give oneself the best care and attention to obtain a sense of ultimate well-being has for some time been perceived to be a selfish practice. For generations people have been conditioned and taught it is inappropriate to pamper or spoil oneself; a concept many have begun to unlearn. We have begun to appreciate that it is our right to put ourselves first, that it is not selfish to claim the best for one's ultimate well-being.

Eventual surrender yields to realising that the best will come about without any fear. But we must learn and develop the art of trust, belief and worthiness. Within this book it is my desire to invite you to practise the art of patience through the healing power of the Angels, the spiritual beings which remain unseen and unheard who are ready to act and help when called.

Signs and Symbols

The symbol of a simple feather began to signify the presence of an Angel while the butterfly signified the presence of the Holy Spirit within me. Initially, after beginning to work with the Angelic realm, I invoked the Angels when I wanted a parking space. It was not enough to think of wanting the Angels to guide me to getting a parking space but rather the importance of vocally calling upon the Angels to help by simply saying: *'Angels, please get me a parking space'* or *'Angels, guide me to a suitable parking space'*, and in most instances I got a suitable car parking space. When a space was not available, it proved to be with patience it came to be or that there was an unforeseen reason why such was not for me.

The next level of testing came about when I prayed for some sign or affirmation regarding a quest at which a feather would fall somewhere within my path. Through time I came to appreciate the great gift bestowed upon me and in my personal space I gave the Angels tasks to undertake on my behalf; I asked the Angels to take what seemed insurmountable to God; I asked the Angels to take the problems of others to Jesus' feet: I began to learn how to surrender. Unceasingly, the healing power of God, which transcended through the Angels, assisted me continuously to believe and share where appropriate my encounters with God's messengers who accompany me day by day. As a consequence of the great gift of God's Heavenly guides, I embrace with love and thankfulness my personal guardian Angel and the Angels who continually work with me, the Angels who respond to me and the Angels who carry my concerns to God.

How do we recognise a sign from above?

How do we determine its legitimacy?

Maybe it is fair to suggest that in some instances it is possible that occurrences are seen as coincident rather than signs. Signs from above may come in various forms: the simplicity of a feather, big or small; a tune or a song that stays with you for a while; not having change at the car park and someone giving you their ticket or a coin; sunshine and birds singing when the winter is at its worst; clouds forming in shapes of Angel wings; rainbows spanning the sky, spreading colours of healing energies and sharing stories with people who have encountered Angels and the healing power of God through the Angels.

Signs and symbols are quite influential within the world of Angels. In various situations signs and symbols provide a positive indication to the presence of God and the energetic sense of Angels. The simple belief and understanding that God accompanies the journey of self is awesome.

The presence of an unseen spiritual being in the form of something as simple as a lone feather can provide a great sense of hope, thus, providing an affirmation that all is well.

*'As an Angel feather fluttered close and tickled
my chilling cheek, I smiled'.*

When one opens oneself to the belief that God's Angels exist, a concept which is and may be difficult for some, there are so many signs and symbols of invitation, love and support given to us often. When we open to the Spirit we become more receptive, the more we open to receive the greater the grace to be aware, accept and acknowledge the powerful energies of God.

The simple image of a lonesome feather can have a profound effect on a person; a symbol is frequently accepted as a sign indicative of the presence of an Angel. In a place where there are no flowers or perfumes, the sweet scent of flowers for many people is associated with the presence of God's Angelic servants. The company of a butterfly can bear resemblance to and the presence of the Holy Spirit, and, the iconic image of the Divine Merciful Jesus whom invites us to trust, to surrender and to embrace the essence of God's eternal love and profound forgiveness offers great hope in abundance.

When I was in Milton Keynes, a young girl challenged the notion that a feather could be a sign of the presence of an Angel. She said, *'You suggest that something as simple as a feather is a sign of an Angel. Well, I have considered that, but, what happens if there are loads of feathers? In my somewhat cynical mind I think, some poor bird has been mauled not that there are loads of Angels around me'.* This young girl had a valid point to make and I could not argue, all I could say was that while she had made a good point, maybe, just maybe depending on what your thought process allows, it is possible that if this happens in an area where there are no threats to creatures of the air, then these feathers are symbolic of a host of Angels. The latter is obviously one which I have encountered, where birds visit regularly and harmoniously feed together. When I was struggling with an uncomfortable situation, every feather meant so much to me, that the notion that a bird may have been attacked didn't even enter my head. As I have been so receptive to this idea, I have come across so many feathers that instead of lifting each one along my path, I pause and quietly say a prayer to my Angel Guardian.

It is so comforting to know that the Angels, God's gift to us, are there to help and assist us. No problem or issue is too small or too large. Archangels can assist a number of people at any one time, Guardian Angels wait with great excitement as their ultimate role is that of bringing happiness and the love of God into our lives. Imagine, being so important. How wonderful it is that we can be assured that there is a powerful healing of God just waiting in the wings, in the wings of this universe, within the wings of the Heavenly beings ready to act under the directive of God, our Saviour.

One day when I was going over to the town, as I approached the lower part of the bridge, a feather danced towards me. As it settled on my bag I lifted it and put it into my pocket. When I looked up, I could see a person whom I do not like to be near me.

I prayed: *'Dear God, please don't let her near me. Please keep her away from me. Immediately without any consideration I began to cross the road. The traffic was heavy but somehow, why I will never know, I found myself standing in the middle of the road between the traffic. A car stopped and I waved to the driver. As I mounted the footpath the other person was roaring across at me. But, I didn't take her on; I just thanked God and my Angel for protecting me and steering me out of the path of negativity'.*

Similarly, when I was in Medjugorje, I encountered a woman who said she had met with what she could only refer to as the devil. She told me *"I know I was going through a dark patch. Everything seemed to be falling apart. I was praying so, so hard. My mum had just died, I was so lonely. The struggle was powerful; I so wanted to believe, I wanted to believe that Mary was there. The more I prayed, the weaker I seemed to be. On the way through the vineyards a man followed behind and caught up with me. He seemed so nice. God it is strange how gullible we can be! Every day we met and went to the Blue Cross where we would recite the rosary. It seemed so good that I had met someone who shared my desire to be healed. At the end of the pilgrimage, when we came home we kept up the friendship. I thought praying together and being there for each other was great until one day out of the blue this person turned on me like a wild animal. My trust had been destroyed. My vulnerability was abused: in my weakness I misinterpreted what I had believed to be friendship, companionship with a soul mate but on the contrary I encountered the spirit of evil"*

Tears were rolling down her cheeks as she continued *"I was so ashamed. I felt abused. I have suffered so much that the positive energies were being destroyed. Oh God, I am ashamed to say this, but I really hate that person. It took me ages to realise that he had the problem not me. And, since becoming aware, accepting and appreciative I have acknowledged the lessons I have received, my spiritual growth is just brilliant. I am so lucky.*

I had a hard time, yes, and it took a long time to recover but I have found such great peace and I am a stronger person than ever. A therapist once said 'be thankful to God for the encounter and the lessons you have learnt. Then release the spirit of that person. Say Goodbye'."

Indeed, sometimes depending on our state of mind it is difficult to decide what is good and what is evil. Angels do come to us when we call. But be careful, as the old story goes: *'Watch out when the chips are down there are always vultures lurking in the distance, ready to strike'.*

There are always those who love to see others brought down; to get their comeuppance, or what they wish upon them. The devil despises those who strive to do their best to achieve the best of what God can give. The devil hates a God-filled soul. The devil will do all in his power to bring the good down. Such can happen as in the case of the devil in the guise of a good companion.

Do not be afraid, God's love is unconditional. Angels do not judge. Angels celebrate when they are included and are allowed to help. Even if we make a mistake, all can be mended when God is allowed to help. It is good to repent. Call upon the Angels of God to protect and guard you, to ward off all evil spirits and keep negative people away from you, your house, your home and your family.

A prayer I say each night: *'God bless and protect our family and friends. Thank you for all the graces and benefits that we as a family have received. Please continue to send your Angels to guard and protect us and to keep all negative spirits away from our house, our home and our family'*. The greatest gift to give God in return is that of the humble forgiveness of the persecutor. This works!

Scriptures and Angels

W ithin scripture there are quite a number of references to Angels, for example within the book of Genesis, 28:12: *"He dreamt that he saw a stairway reaching from earth to heaven with Angels going up and down from it"*. This simple reference provides an image of *'out of this world existence'* and the activity of God's agents, Angels. Likewise, when Isaac prepared an altar upon which he was ready to lay his son as an offering to God, such an extreme submission was prohibited when an Angel appeared. Archangel Gabriel appeared to Mary bringing the Good News that she was the chosen one who in humility would accept what God asked of her. . . .

Angels are Messengers and agents of God. Within Scripture there is a number of relevant citings in relation to Angels, the messengers and agents of God and of Heaven. Beginning with the Old Testament, (OT) Angels, the messengers and agents of God are to be revealed in the Book of Genesis, Numbers, Kings, Chronicles, Zechariah and the Psalms. Within the New Testament (NT) associated references may be sourced, within the Gospels of Matthew, Luke, and John, also in the Acts of the Apostles, the Book of Thessalonians, Hebrews and Revelations.

In relation to Angels and Heaven, such sources may be found in the NT, in the Gospels of Matthew and

Luke, Letters to the Colossians, Timothy, and the Book of Revelations. References to *'Angel of the Lord'* can be found in the OT, the Book of Genesis, Exodus, and Judges. Guardian Angels are referenced within the OT, in the Psalms and in the Books of Isaiah and Daniel and in the Gospel of Matthew, NT; while the concept of guiding Angels is referenced in the OT, within the Book of Genesis, Exodus, Numbers and Judges.

Generally, we wish to think of the Angels as all gentle, good and nice, it is important that we acknowledge that there are Angels of evil, fallen Angels; destroying Angels. Such references are to be sourced as destroying Angels mentioned in the OT, within the Book of Samuel, Kings, Chronicles, Isaiah and the Psalms and in the Acts of the Apostles, NT.

Many references appear in relation to Satan, the devil, the evil one, the fallen Angels in the NT: in the Gospel of Matthew, Letters to the Corinthians, Jude and the Book of Revelations. Indeed, this list is not exhausted as there are so many references to mention.

Aspects of Angels

W hile in a historical and traditional belief, this spiritual element of self can be nourished first and foremost as a consequence of spiritual in–dwelling. Christian baptism and integration into a Christian living community is a gift of grace. In the absence of practice there is a void, no sense of belonging. For some people it may appear easy to feel that life can be lived without such a spiritual support, while on the other hand there may be people who don't feel worthy of such spiritual support.

The well-being of the soul yields fruit in plenty and performs best with the help and support given through the power of the Holy Spirit, the guidance of Church and with the healing energies of the Messengers of God. The energy of all three are available to all who call, trust and believe. Just as any process, to gain knowledge, to learn and to believe involves patience and confidence to trust and believe. These considerations cannot be turned on and off like a tap but grow with determination and perseverance.

As mentioned earlier, until very recently there were only three Archangels frequently called upon, Archangels Michael, Raphael and Gabriel. . . . Each of these Archangels has a specific role to play in relation to needs of God's creation, which includes all aspects of life and living. It is important to remember that Angels, Archangels and

Ascended Masters serve to please God. They intercede on our behalf; therefore, we do not worship or adore these spiritual beings.

Angels are not magical, they are not fairies, and they have specific roles to carry out for the highest good of each soul. The notion of Angels is not an airy fairy affair. In life and living there are no barriers except those we help to construct or allow others to create. Barriers can be broken, it is our responsibility to acknowledge the power of the Angels and how they can serve to help us dismantle the blockages which negatively impact on life and living.

Personal Angel Journey

As a child I remember Angels being quite an important feature in my life. The beautiful and fanciful image of a tall young female with beautiful long hair dressed in a long flowing garment, enveloped in a huge pair of feathered wings still lives in my mind. On awakening in the morning and preparing to go to bed at night my parents never failed to invoke the Angels; we fervently called upon the Angels to guard and protect us all, my siblings, my parents and myself.

One night, when I was about six years old, I was feeling hard done by and was a little weepy; the room was so dark. I was under the blankets crying when all of a sudden a vast bright light shone over the far wall. I remember being scared but curious, dipping in and out from the bed clothes. I saw a tall figure, couldn't say at first whether it was male or female. The figure was dressed in a warrior outfit with a copper breast plate and a long sparkling sword. Imagine, I couldn't make up my mind whether this figure was that of a man or a woman. I never forgot this image despite that, as a child, the vision didn't mean much until one night when we were watching a film about Joan of Arc, I became so excited as I recognised this to be the Angel who came to me, the image reflected that of the spirit who came to me, the armoured breastplate shone just like the one the Angel wore. It made sense, I couldn't make up my mind if the figure was male or female; Joan of Arc was a girl, she wore a soldiers' outfit, her hair was short!

Yet, I remember, there was something extraordinary about this, I was excited and yet I was confused. When we were young, if something could not be explained it was easier for an adult to suggest that it was a figment of your imagination and it would be better to forget about it . . . . I didn't forget. Even all these years later, every time I watch the film, *'The Story of Joan of Arc'* I fondly remember the night I believed she appeared to me.

And this rekindles the image of us, the family, gathered together to pray; we recited the well learnt prayer to our Angel Guardian, in a lilting happy tone as with great belief we knew our Angel Guardian would not only listen but would be a great protector. This tradition of teaching and reciting of this invocation, this powerful prayer for the guidance and protection of our Guardian Angel continues to be important. The gentle morning and night invocation which I refer to is simply called the *'Prayer to Our Angel Guardian'* or *'Angel of God'* and goes simply as follows:

'Angel of God, my guardian dear, to whom God's love commits me here; ever this day/night be at my side, to light, to guard, to rule and guide. Amen.'

As a child, I remember very clearly a story which my mum had told many people. I was nearly six years old and my brother was almost five. As usual we were sent off to school which was a short distance away. It was raining really heavily. Instead of going on to school my brother and I stood under the great sprawling sycamore tree at the bottom of the school grounds, for shelter.

We really believed that it was Jesus and not the tree which was keeping us dry. Jesus put a huge red cloak around us. As we huddled together, a neighbour passing by saw us and insisted on taking us back home. My mummy's immediate reaction was that we were skiving, (which wasn't the case!). Without any hesitation we excitedly told mummy that we saw Jesus: *'He was so beautiful. He was wearing a flowing red cloak which he put around us while we stood in under the tree out of the rain. Then we saw sparkling lights as the rain fell. And Jesus said; tell your mummy I will call to see the twins'.* Mummy was having none of it. She was angry and got ready to take us down to school. And as she did, I can still hear Mrs Campbell saying *'Maybe they did see Jesus?'* As we were marched down to the school, Sister Pascal, the School Principal, a tall thin nun, calm and gentle in her approach, came to meet us.

After listening to my mummy's story she put her arms around us and asked us to tell her the story of good news and again with great excitement we told her that Jesus was calling up to see the twins. I can remember her sweet smile of quiet approval. When I approached Sister Ursula's classroom, second room at the far end of the corridor, I opened the classroom door, the class were just reciting the prayer to the Angels. It is strange how things stay in your mind, and how even the smallest things can impact upon life.

Even as an adult, every time I recite this prayer the image of a beautiful heavenly being becomes so clear and ever present. This spiritual Angelic presence, however, while very powerful within my childhood years was a conceptual image that slipped out of sight, indeed even out of mind for a time through my youth when I became self absorbed and independent. The unintentional easing out of God occurred. I was too busy with life and living and didn't embrace the idea of or for Angels. *That was a childish idea!*

Despite saying the prayer consistently on a daily basis throughout all my early childhood life, the image and the relevance of the Angels did not impact greatly on my life and living until quite recently. I guess one of the reasons for such a confession is affected by the somewhat gentle and unobtrusive manner in which we relied upon the Angels. I suppose, the emphasis was not extraordinarily applied to Angels.

We could not comprehend how powerful Angels really were within the context of support. In actual fact, there was little mention as to how active Angels were; we didn't have the capacity of understanding to be able to appreciate their impact and influence in relation to our spiritual development and consequential wellbeing.

After all, initially it was quite simple: we were taught that we had a Guardian Angel, we were taught to pray to our Guardian Angel but that seemed to be *that*. Within contemporary society, we are encouraged to appreciate and develop a healthy interest and relationship with Angels as spiritual friends and acknowledge the healing power of the Angels and their impact upon our daily life and living.

When the concept of Angels was being discussed and indeed debated, I was quietly intrigued but weary of how such fitted in with the Church's teaching. While it is clear that Angels were mentioned frequently within the Scriptures, 'Angels' were not talked about to any great extent, as they are and continue to be addressed in recent times. Indeed, the reawakening of the concept of Angels had gained great attention to the extent that God in many cases was been pushed aside.

As time has passed, this is not so much the case, as the meaning of Angels as Messengers of God is now greatly emphasised and acknowledged. There has been an avalanche of material produced relating to the topic of *'Angels'* and their purpose. Angel cards have been designed and many images have been painted, with the fundamental focus on the realisation that Angels are of God.

Within the various religions and faith traditions, the Heavenly cosmos is acknowledged, Angels are regarded as messengers of God, they are the heavenly beings who assist us in our quest for God's help and support. Very often it is the spiritual path of life which is somewhat neglected. Life and life's experiences often dominate the path of life and living, a journey which is unique to each of us. The human and basic needs of individuals irrespective of religion, colour or creed focus on the need for ultimate wellbeing.

The superficial and complex needs of self can very easily be neglected, such in turn usually manifests itself in some negative form, for some this may be physical, for others it may be psychological. Physical and mental illness affect most of us at some point in time; indeed for some the occurrence can be overwhelming and overbearing but in most cases, traditional forms of medical support and medicine have been the norm in endeavouring to mend the brokenness of self.

However, over the last decade and more, people have become more medically aware, more accountable and responsible for their own wellbeing and have become more open to new approaches to attaining and sustaining ultimate wellbeing.

Fix it, Fix what?

For many of us, it is a human trait to believe that we can fix everything, and if we cannot then we are a failure, we are useless, worthless and so on. This is not so, this concept is one of self. Very often the ego seeks much attention. We try too hard and in the midst of our endeavours we lose sight of the greater aspect of life, the spiritual dimension of being. For many it's almost as if God doesn't even exist and the ego strives to take control. The possible conflict of everyday life and living can allow us to fall victim to the belief that we must *'fix it'. Fix what? But fix what?*

Sometimes, we even try to fix that which is not broken. If we continue to fight such a battle eventually negativity will take centre stage of our lives, and be allowed to begin to further corrupt the inner peace of being. We can begin to feel and believe that we are inept, incompetent individuals if we can't change and mend every situation and solve not only our own problems but everyone else's as well!

The aftermath of such a negative experience can only serve to be detrimental to one's ultimate well-being, as the body, mind and soul are affected. As in the words of St. Paul: *'when one part suffers all parts suffer'*. The challenge is to look beyond the temporary fix; the material aspect of wellbeing, the bottom line is that wholeness of self cannot occur if all parts are not equally attended to: no one part is more worthy of help than the other. Therefore, we are invited to seek wellbeing in its totality. Through God and the Angels, alongside Physical and Psychological therapies, wholeness of self can be achieved.

Through many, not so pleasant encounters with people, many issues in need of assistance quite often are beyond our remit and our personal ability and capability to help, but, we don't always either realise this to be so, or accept such to be true. It is humbling to know that we cannot fix everything and that it is alright to accept that we are not as powerful human beings as we believe we are, or want to be or ought to be.

It's healthy to recognise our needs.

But why stop there?

Act and seek help!

When we call upon the Angels with full trust and belief, it is then that we can begin to accept and appreciate that there are things we cannot change; we begin to realise and accept the courage and understanding to surrender everything to the Angels. After which we will experience and learn to embrace the healing power of the Angels, a heavenly healing which is for everyone. The healing power of God is brought to us by the Heavenly Messengers who are always ready and waiting to help. Just call!

Angels come in various forms, that's true; sometimes at the most unexpected times, places, and in images that only make sense at a later time. There is no such thing as *'I can't; I should have; I couldn't etc.'* We all have the gift of *'free will'*, *'freedom of choice'*.

Angels are present when there is:

a chill that cannot be explained;
a warmth that cannot be explained;
a presence that cannot be explained;
a voice that cannot be explained;
a ray of light shines through the darkness!
a tinkle, a chime is heard;
a twinkle of light appears;
an orb of brilliant light transmits messages of God.

We must never forget that the Angels are representative of God, sometimes they may take on a human form when visiting earth, therefore, be cautious, be alert to witness that Angels are with us: *"Do not forget to show hospitality to strangers, for by so doing people have shown hospitality to angels without knowing it."* Hebrews 13:2. It is also important to note that while Angels are ranked higher than man, they are ranked below God. Therefore, they are not to be worshipped or adored. Angels wait to serve.

'Angels do come—Just call!'

Meditation And Prayer

Meditative Exercise

When in need, when tired, distressed:

*T*ry this exercise: light a candle—close your eyes.
Take three deep breaths. Patiently relax.
Wait. Just rest in the Spirit of God.
Lights emerge—maybe white powerful and acute.
Shimmer rays of green and blue lights fusing together bringing healing and strength.
Embrace the colours vibrant and bold, circling and twirling, bringing vitality and energy. Absorb the presence of peace, tranquillity.
Rest in the ambience embodied in love, hope and peace.
Gently, let go. Listen to what it is Jesus wants to say to you. Rest, relax.
When ready count backwards from ten.
Slowly breathe in and out three times.
Open your eyes and slowly adjust to the light.
Rise slowly. Take a drink of water.
Bank the experience.
When in need of comfort or support return to this simple exercise and renew your energy.

Kate O'Kane

Angels gather round me!

Angels gather round me,
embalm me with your love,
Let me know that God has sent
a guide to watch o'er me!
In the depth of fear and pain,
let me know you're near:
Wrap me in the cloak of peace
made of Angel dust.
Angels gather round me,
even when all is well
Let me call aloud with hope
and accept God's gift of love.
Angel, never leave me,
let me know you're close
So with great love and tender care,
I'll embrace God's gift to me.
Angels gather round me,
never leave me 'ere I pray
Hear my silent words of need
Let me know you care;
I am assured that I'll be secure,
today and everyday:
For God has chosen to give to me,
a guardian for my care.
Angels gather round me,
I embrace you with great love.
Heavenly beings who'll walk with me
and lift me when I fall;
Your awesome presence is surreal;
I know God chose with care
Some Guardians Angels to care for me,
Through each day and night!

As my youngest grand-daughter, Caomihe told me, after a sleep over: *'granny, last night when I was in Roisin's bed, the Angels where flying around the roof, there were twinkling lights and the Angels were singing out loud, 'bualadh bos'* which is Irish for *'clap your hands/round of applause'*.

So I wish to dedicate this prayer to my grandchildren,

Cristiona, Cormac and Caomihe

Prayer to our Guardian Angel

Angel of God, my guardian dear,
to whom God's love commits me here:
ever this day be at my side,
to light and guard, to rule and guide, Amen.

Prayer to St. Michael
the Archangel

St. Michael the Archangel, defend us in the day of battle; Be our safeguard against the wickedness and snares of the Devil. May God rebuke Him, we humbly pray, and do thou, O Prince of the Heavenly Host, by the power of God, cast into Hell, Satan and all the other evil spirits, who prowl through the world, seeking the ruin of souls. Amen.

Chaplet to
St. Michael the Archangel

Act of Sorrow, Reconciliation
Promises of St. Michael

Whosoever would practice this devotion in his honour would have, when approaching the Holy Table, an escort of nine Angels chosen from each of the nine choirs. In addition, for the daily recital of these nine salutations he promised his continual assistance and that all the Holy Angels during life, and after death deliverance from purgatory for themselves and their relations.

Recitation of the Chaplet

O God, come to my assistance.
O Lord, make haste to help me.

Glory be to the Father, and to the Son and to the Holy Spirit, as it was in the beginning is now and ever shall be, world without end, Amen.

Say one Our Father and three Hail Marys after each of the nine salutations.

1. By the intercession of St. Michael and the celestial Choir of Seraphim, may the Lord make us worthy to burn with the fire of perfect charity. Amen.
2. By the intercession of St. Michael and the celestial Choir of Cherubim, may the Lord vouchsafe to grant us grace to leave the ways of wickedness to run in the paths of Christian perfection. Amen
3. By the intercession of St. Michael and the celestial Choir of Thrones, may the Lord infuse into our hearts a true and sincere spirit of humility. Amen.
4. By the intercession of St. Michael and the celestial Choir of Dominions, may the Lord give us grace to govern our senses and subdue our unruly passions. Amen.
5. By the intercession of St. Michael and the celestial Choir of Powers, may the Lord vouchsafe to protect our souls against the snare and temptations of the devil. Amen.
6. By the intercession of St. Michael and the celestial Choir of Virtues, may the Lord preserve us from evil and suffer us not to fall into temptation. Amen.
7. By the intercession of St. Michael and the celestial Choir of Principalities, may God fill our souls with a true spirit of obedience. Amen.
8. By the intercession of St. Michael and the celestial Choir of Archangels, may the Lord give us perseverance in faith and in all good works, in order that we gain the glory of Paradise. Amen.

9. By the intercession of St. Michael and the celestial Choir of Angels, may the Lord grant us to be protected by them in this mortal life and conducted hereafter to eternal glory. Amen.

10. Recite one Our Father in honour of each of the leading Angels:

St. Michael; St. Raphael; St. Gabriel, and your Guardian Angel.

O Glorious Prince St. Michael, chief and commander of the Heavenly Hosts, guardian of souls, vanquisher of rebel spirits, servant in the house of the Divine King, and our admirable conductor, thou who dost shine with excellence and superhuman virtue, vouchsafe to deliver us from all evil, who turn to Thee with confidence, and enable us by thy gracious protection to serve God more and more faithfully every day.

Pray for us, O glorious St. Michael, Prince of the Church of Jesus Christ, that we may be made worthy of His promises.

Use these prayers in time of need, in time of thanksgiving, in time of stress, worry or loneliness. Prayers are for every one's use irrespective of faith tradition; everyone has *free will, free choice* to seek help.

Angels do come—Just Call!

About the author

Kate O'Kane lives in Northern Ireland and is married with three grown up children and three beautiful grand children. In earlier adult years she managed a Boutique which led her to many trips to London. Later in life she has struggled with ill health which has caused her to give up a career in Educational Administration and Finance. But, *'as the saying goes when one door closes another door opens'* and she found writing, poetry and prose, a therapeutic, challenging and enjoyable outlet to her condition. She also returned to university as a mature student where she gained a Degree in Psychology. This led to further studies in Theology and Spirituality. Through periods of illness she has explored the alternative and complementary therapies. As a practising Roman Catholic, she owns a profound sense of Spirituality. She knows all about the sorrows and joys of everyday life. She continues to embrace life in whatever form or guise it may appear. This is reflected in her insightful and thoughtful writing which she wishes to share as a source of comfort and awareness of Angels.